DREAM MADLY, PURSUE WILDLY, AND TRUST COMPLETELY™:

What You Wanted to Be When You Grew Up

CHARLOTTE D. HUNT

Dream Madly Publishing

Praise For

*DREAM MADLY, PURSUE WILDLY, AND TRUST COMPLETELY™:
WHAT YOU WANTED TO BE WHEN YOU GREW UP*

"Destined to be a Best Seller and a must read if you have even an ounce of ambition and drive left in your soul."

- **Actor Nick Mancuso and pro golfer Greg Martin**
Mancuso-Martin Entertainment

"This book reads more like an uplifting sermon in life's lessons than a guide book. Drawing from her own experiences along with thousands of others, the author lays out a step-by-step plan to help you conquer your demons and fears in order to pursue your dreams. For those out there without hope or dreams...read this book."

- **Bill Cuomo**
Dove and Grammy award winning arranger, writer, producer, and keyboardist

"Having a dream is essential for enjoying lifelong happiness. Charlotte does a wonderful job communicating this and so much more in her new book. By the time you finish reading, 'Dream Madly, Pursue Wildly, Trust Completely,' you should have no question as to the benefits of taking the author's advice in order to live a more meaningful and joyful life"

- **Ricky Powell**
Supervising Network Associate Director at NBC Universal, Inc.

"Finally someone who can explain why I feel so uncomfortable being "normal". I am a dreamer. If you believe that about yourself, read this book. It will help you learn how to dream like you did when you were a child, pursue the dream like your life depended on it, and trust that the pursuit is worth it even when it seems otherwise."

- **Renita Walker**
Chaplain, St. Luke's Hospital

"Author Charlotte Hunt knows what it's like to dream. She challenges us to rekindle our dreams, pursue them with gusto, and see them fulfilled as we trust in the Dream-Giver Himself. Don't miss this book! It will rejuvenate you, even as it calls to your heart to come along for the journey."

- **Kathi Macias**
Award-winning novelist and author of *Red Ink* (www.kathimacias.com)

"There are some books that come along that compel the reader to find out how it ends – this is one of those books, except it ends whenever the reader decides – and that is what makes this book unique! This book has reawakened my desire to dream, and dream big enough to fail! Thank you for sharing a part of your story, so that I can continue mine!!"

- **Estella V., Louisville, KY**

"I just finished reading your book and I just couldn't put it down. You kept me on the edge of my chair with each page. At times bringing me to complete tears, and other times laughter, but at the same time motivating me and encouraging me along the way! After reading your book I feel I can rise up out of my box and dream, dreams big enough to fail! You make me want to write my story. I can't wait till your next book!"

Sharon F. Akron, OH

FOREWORD BY NICK MANCUSO & DR. GREG MARTIN

DREAM MADLY, PURSUE WILDLY, AND TRUST COMPLETELY™

WHAT YOU WANTED TO BE WHEN YOU GREW UP

CHARLOTTE D. HUNT

Dream Madly Publishing

DREAM MADLY, PURSUE WILDLY, AND TRUST COMPLETELY™:
WHAT YOU WANTED TO BE WHEN YOU GREW UP

Published by Dream Madly Publishing
Plano, TX 75093
Copyright © 2012 by Charlotte D. Hunt

ISBN-10: 0615599400
ISBN-13: 978-0615599403
Printed in the United States of America

Cover and Interior Design: Charlotte D. Hunt
Edited: Jim Kavanagh

All rights reserved. No part of this book may be reproduced, stored in a retrieval system, transmitted in any form or by any means - electronic, mechanical, photocopy, or otherwise - without written permission from Dream Madly Productions except for brief quotations in printed reviews.

All Scripture quotations from the New American Standard Bible®, Copyright © 1960, 1962, 1963, 1968, 1971, 1972, 1973, 1975, 1977, 1995 by The Lockman Foundation. Used by permission (www.Lockman.org).

Merriam-Webster Online Dictionary copyright © 2012 by Merriam-Webster, Inc. (www.Merriam-Webster.com)

Details in some anecdotes and stories have been changed to protect the identities of the persons involved.

Disclaimer

Nothing written in this book, or exercises contained therein should replace the advice and counsel of a treatment professional specializing in your specific needs. I not only encourage seeking the counsel of a licensed therapist but also endorse that relationship with someone whom you can work with in person.

TABLE OF CONTENTS

PREFACE: The Survey xi
FOREWORD by Nick Mancuso & Greg Martin xvii
ACKNOWLEDGEMENTS xxiii

Chapter 1   What If? 27
Chapter 2   What You Wanted To Be When You Grew Up 35
Chapter 3   To Dream Madly: The Path Less Taken 49
Chapter 4   Beginning to Dream Again 59
Chapter 5   Dream Stealer #1-Fear 65
Chapter 6   Dream Stealer #2-The Past 81
Chapter 7   Dream Stealer #3-Emotions 93
Chapter 8   Dream Stealer #4-People 105
Chapter 9   Dream Stealer #5-Performance 119
Chapter 10 Pursuing Wildly: The Journey Feared 133
Chapter 11 Trusting Completely: The Waiting Game 149
Chapter 12 A Dream From Your Story 165
Chapter 13 Purpose: Living A Life That Matters 179
Chapter 14 Exercises & Worksheets 187

NOTES 199
THE AUTHOR 208

PREFACE

THE SURVEY

The French poet Charles Baudelaire once wrote, "The devil's best trick is to persuade you that he doesn't exist." I will take it a step further and state, "The greatest plan Satan ever pulled was cutting off people's potential by believing a lie." Let's face it: He is outstanding at his job and is winning ... hands down.

He wins daily through lies in the lives of some of the rich and famous who believe their potential is limited to outrageous acts or use of their wealth that will gain a precious fifteen minutes of the spotlight instead of holding out for lifetime dreams.

He wins hourly through lies in the lives of some of the abused, battered, and outcasts who believe their dreams and hopes are out of reach due to the scars and imperfections of their past and mistakes made.

He also wins moment by moment through lies in the lives of everyday people who believe their dreams, visions, and hopes should be placed on the shelf or forgotten because of unemployment, world issues, age, family situations and current circumstances that seem more powerful than their future.

He certainly won in the life of my father, a man who had great ideas and dreams but allowed the dream stealers in his life to snatch away every single dream and hope he had. He was a master printer and the king of the sanguine temperament. My father could make a stranger feel like a best friend within fifteen minutes of meeting them and have the person pledging their loyalty to the relationship within the hour.

I remember him telling me of a dream he had to head his own print and copy business. He longed to succeed where his own father failed and earn his place as head of the house where my mother dominated.

Over a period of years, my father began to realize his dream of being a business owner and started a small shop with his cousin on the outskirts of town. At the moment he was to finalize his dream, he succumbed to the dream stealers of his fears, past, emotions, people and his believed lack of performance and walked away leaving his cousin to continue on with his own business dream.

My father died in 1995 from alcoholism and liver failure, alone, penniless, separated from his family, jobless, and regretful of the great offenses and mistakes of his past. He never reached the most important dream and goal of his life. His dream never happened because of the choices he made and giving in to the dream stealers in his life. He believed a lie.

For some, the lie is the hurtful curse of a father saying, "You will never amount to anything!" For some, the lie is remembering the time when failure came through a business loss, divorce, lost relationship, rejection, or an organizational mishap. Others hold onto a lie of fear that haunts them about their inadequacies, believed obstacles, limitations, outcomes, misplaced feelings and judgments about themselves.

Still, others have no major fears, obstacles, or believed limitations in their way. They simply are comfortable in settling for the obtainable and remaining safe and ordinary in a life that requires little effort, risk or pursuit.

During the summer of 2010, I surveyed 2,034 people to evaluate their beliefs and values regarding dreams and hope. Through their responses to the sixty statements, I wanted to see if people (representing a cross-section of racial, gender, religious, social and class status) were dreaming for the future, moving toward their potential, hopeful in their lives, and pursuing and trusting in the idea that their life mattered and made a difference.

Three amazing results came from that non-scientific survey. First, regardless of their background or culture, people carried similar beliefs and skewed filters regarding themselves and the world around them.

Second, eighty-eight percent of people taking the survey stated fear and failure as the number one reason for not dreaming or pursuing their dreams or visions.

The third and most heartbreaking conclusion was ninety percent stated either their past or present situation or something they viewed as an inadequacy in themselves (education, age, worth, ability, inexperience, etc.) was an obstacle in trusting and pursuing their dreams.

Despite success, class, religion, wealth, or fame, people believed their lives held little value for greatness outside of what they could perform or possess. Many asked, "How do I dream and hope for the future despite my past and current situations and world crisis all around?"

Motivational talks of positive thinking, name it and claim it, stab it and grab it were not working. Infomercials teaching people to simply dream and be a better person were not working. Something needed to be done. I decided to write a book.

"Dream Madly, Pursue Wildly, Trust Completely™: What You Wanted to Be When You Grew Up", is a personal development frontal assault for those who have seemingly run out of tactical options to recapture a child-like freedom in pursuing their hopes, visions and dreams toward a life that matters. This book is an encouragement guide and manual filled with exercises, stories of true-life dreamers, diagrams, personal experiences, and clinical assistance in discovering the dreams and purposes placed in us while understanding our life stories. It is a mirror to reflect the fact that we, as a society, stopped dreaming, pursuing, and trusting for our future and a hope that has not arrived yet.

"Dream Madly, Pursue Wildly, Trust Completely™: What You Wanted to Be When You Grew Up" answers the question, "How do I dream and hope for the future despite the past or the current situations I am living out? In short, this book is a motivating guide to help dreamers in their journey to dreaming madly, pursuing wildly, and trusting completely™ in spite of past or present feelings or situations.

My second book, award winning, *"Damaged Goods: Learning to Dream Again"* was about realizing a wonderful plan and purpose for our lives in spite of our past, current situations, and views of how we believe our lives should have been lived out until now. The book helped to understand that our stories and lives have purpose regardless of what we go through.

This book meets us where so many are today in the journey toward the dreams, visions, and future placed in us. We are walking out that journey but we are getting tired and frustrated, desiring to give up, put the dream on the shelf and resign ourselves to the dream stealers that are part of the journey. We are not crazy, mixed up or weird. We simply need direction and encouragement for our journey.

Please note that nothing written in this book or exercises contained in it should replace the advice and counsel of a treatment professional specialized for your specific needs. I not only encourage seeking the counsel of a licensed therapist but also endorse that relationship with someone whom you can work with in person.

Join me as we journey together to unleash your power and potential to Dream Madly, Pursue Wildly, and Trust Completely™.

FOREWORD BY
NICK MANCUSO & GREG MARTIN

Rest assured Charlotte Hunt's book will change your life- and we are humbled and greatly honored to be asked to write its foreword.

We first noticed Charlotte a year ago through a social media site. Daily she would post messages of encouragement and exhortations to push toward dreams without regard to believed limitations. We watched as her followers and friends gravitated to her honesty and vulnerability. They gained insights and anticipated her words for the next day's post or blog. People drew to her and felt the closeness of a sister and friend instead of a stranger who offered encouragement and support from her own life experiences and counseling background.

As time passed, we were drawn in by Charlotte's personal support of our dreams and projects and the prayers for situations that occurred in our lives. Surely, this was no ordinary woman. The more we grew to know about her, the more we were astonished by her heart and passion to see people begin to dream for their lives and identify the issues that were preventing them from reaching their potential. We were amazed at her positive and hopeful attitude considering her past and the tremendous obstacles she has faced in her lifetime:

- Sexually abused by seven abusers between eighteen months and sixteen years old
- Physically abused by her mother-still carries physical scars
- Told by a pastor that God would never use her because she was damaged goods
- Battled depression and great sense of worthlessness
- Endured eating and drug addiction
- Battled hopelessness to the point of seven suicide attempts
- Disabled physically by age twenty-eight by advanced rheumatoid arthritis

Charlotte Hunt understands what it means to have dreams tossed to the side and to give up her dreams due to the lies and bondage of her past. She knows the pain of failing miserably and then rising to take another step, and falling down again. Charlotte knows the betrayal of trust and the hardship of misplaced trust. However, she also understands what it means to dream again and to "dream, dreams big enough to fail." She knows the joy of crossing the finish line after taking the final steps of pursuit despite past failings. Charlotte knows the rest of trusting and hoping in the face of harm, struggle, and fear.

We have experienced Charlotte's great gift of inspiration and encouragement, which touches everyone. She understands life and lives it joyously and wonderfully. Charlotte's life is a testimony that screams, "Dreams and hope are available to anyone, without limitation."

Her life and the inspiration she offers people through her presentations cannot be bottled. However, the next best thing is through the pages of this book. We believe that Charlotte's unique insight will provide readers with a new perspective and lease on life to dream and hope. Her book takes her encouragement, life's work, counseling experience, and great knowledge of dreaming, pursuing, and trusting and places it in practical form for others to grow and dream.

We've always believed that without our dreams, we are bound to run in circles. Goals and dreams have always played a major role in our lives. In the words of Charlotte's book, we had to *"Dream Madly, Pursue Wildly, and Trust Completely."* With over 300 films and 40 years in Hollywood and many years in various businesses and professional golf, we have dreamed, had successes and failures. We also recognize that it is only the "good stories well told" that impact the audience to make a difference in their lives. Charlotte has truly achieved this milestone.

We highly recommend Charlotte, this book, and everything she has written to take stock of your life, your goals and dreams. You might just end up meeting some very interesting people, starring in a movie, running for political office, or being a great writer and educator just like Charlotte Hunt.

Greg Martin & Nick Mancuso - 2011
Mancuso-Martin Entertainment - Fort Worth, Texas

To Jack Kavanagh and Those Who Have Dreamt Madly

Thank you for your example and courage in showing us the journey of one who Dreams Madly. You took steps of courage, made mistakes, fell down, stood up, refocused, then took another step, questioning the difficulty of the journey, but never the potential of the dream. You were not men and women who were special or extraordinary, just simple people who longed for more and encouraged us to be anything but ordinary. Thank you for your writings, inventions, accomplishments, stories, industries, breakthroughs, legacies … and dreams.

ACKNOWLEDGEMENTS

**To my agent, my assistant, Diane Harper,
and my management team:**

Thank you for believing in me and making my life easier so I can pour my energy into creating work from my heart and life's passion. You are too wonderful.

**To Saundra Dalton Smith, Pastor Cleveland Moore, Esther Shuman,
Melody Earle, Diane Markins, Bryant Scott,
Tess Wolfe, and Kathi Macias:**

I will forever be in your debt. I can never thank you enough for your support, help, encouragement, prayers, suggestions, and laughter. I was only able to complete this book because of you. Thank you.

To my editor, Jim Kavanagh:

Words will never express my thankfulness, and appreciation for you. Thank you so much for support, suggestions, shoulders, great writing, and just being there.

To Terry Fairfax:

We have traveled many years and different roads together and apart. I recall some of my most favorite and funniest moments with you on the bandstand. In all your imperfections, you are one of the finest men and musicians I know. I am grateful and honored to call you my friend. I love you sincerely.

To my friends, blog readers, FB supporters, and buddies

You have no idea how much you mean to me. Thank you for your feedback, ideas, wall posts, humor, support, prayers, and reality checks.
I do what I do because you are there.

To my Father God, and Savior, Jesus Christ:

Thanks for the safety, rest, and comfort of your lap, the grace of your love, and for being the greatest dreamer who ever lived.
Thank you for restoring my dreams.

CHAPTER ONE

WHAT IF?

"God Almighty has set before me two great objects, the suppression of the slave trade and the reformation of manners (morality)".

---- William Wilberforce (1759–1833)

I will never forget the day I went to the movie theatre to see *Amazing Grace*. My mother had passed months earlier of pancreatic cancer in the fall of 2006 and I desperately needed a distraction from the work, worry, pressure, and grief of my life.

Although I realized the movie was inspired by the true story of William Wilberforce, I knew little about the legacy of his life or the journey he experienced to reach his deepest longings and dreams. Wilberforce was a late-blooming Christian who lived in Britain during the nineteenth century and was involved with the slave trade. That information piqued my interest enough for me to go to the movies and spend the better part of my paycheck at the concession stand.

As I chomped through my bucket of popcorn, I discovered Wilberforce was a member of the British Parliament who campaigned against the British slave trade for twenty-six years until the passage of the Slave Trade Act in 1807. He was wealthy, hedonistic in his early life, sickly, uninterested in studying in college, and had to be coaxed into politics by his friend, William Pitt.

Wilberforce was not a man looking to change the world by following a dream, but he did. His dream began over dinner on

March 13, 1787, when a gathering of abolitionists asked Wilberforce to lead the parliamentary campaign to abolish the slave trade in Britain.

My heart pounded as I grew to know more about the great figure and the risks and challenges he faced. Soon, I began to witness the journey of a man who became determined toward a dream and knew he was the one assigned for the task. As I watched, I began to have hope and renewed strength for my own life.

His story contained many themes, intersections, experiences, and friends that would ultimately direct the path and passion of his dream. However, he was neither ready nor willing to walk toward that dream until the age of twenty-eight. By the end of his life on July 29, 1833, at age seventy-three, Wilberforce had forever changed the world and affected lives because he had followed a single dream.

His one dream spawned other dreams and acts that created the Society for the Prevention of Cruelty to Animals and the establishment of a free colony in Sierra Leone (a dream that was of an ideal society in which races would mix on equal terms).

Days before his death, a campaign was launched that led to the Slavery Abolition Act of 1833. William Wilberforce's dream became a reality.

I went to the movie for a needed escape, but I left the theatre more convinced than ever that our dreams and visions are not about accomplishments, reaching goals, or even obtaining success. Our dreams and visions change our lives, establish a purpose for our placement on earth, and impact the lives of others and the world in whatever territory or capacity has been ordained for us.

So often, we see movies, witness stories of others' lives, and find ourselves left in awe of their accomplishments, risks, and sacrifices. Then we step back, review our own lives, and become disappointed with the dreams we have kept hidden. We wonder about the possibilities and if we had taken the road less traveled in moving toward our hopes and dreams.

WHAT IF?

Have you ever looked out of a window on a beautiful summer's day and thought about what could have been? Have you ever read or watched a biography and desired to live your life with a similar purpose and calling? Have you ever witnessed a wrong, discovered a need, had a passion that stirred inside your heart, or felt drawn toward a specific path or direction and knew some way, somehow you were meant to do something about it?

If you have ever felt those things, perhaps you were facing something many people desire but few walk out. You were challenged to dream, to stretch yourself beyond what was reasonable, expected, and ordinary. If you have ever felt those things, perhaps now is your time to begin or continue walking forward in pursuing the purpose, calling, dreams, and visions placed in you.

Each of us has a story. There is no such thing as a "worthless life." Whether your dream is to have an active and abundant life through your family, friends, and neighbors; to start a ministry to serve a certain population, community, or need; or to be a writer, actor, speaker, teacher, preacher, salesperson, office worker, visionary, leader, or servant, it is to yours to live out.

Our dreams are for Dreaming Madly, Pursuing Wildly, and Trusting Completely. Having a dream is a precious gift that needs to be protected and fought for. However, having a dream also means a journey must take place worthy of the dream that will take us through a land of learning, waiting, sacrifice, storytelling, pursuing, trusting, and finding hope that will leave us breathless.

I have experienced three types of people in my work: those who never thought about their dreams and are considering the possibility; those who have thought about their dreams and have deep desires to rekindle them; and those who have placed their dreams on the back burner and struggle to begin to dream again. The questions to ponder are these: Do you have a story to tell and share and are you willing to dream?

Some have said it is better not to dream than to dream and not succeed. Although that statement is understandable from a failing point of view, it speaks nothing to success and the road to greatness, which comes from mistakes. Dreaming requires the acceptance that at some point, there will be a mistake, an unmet deadline, and plans that won't match up to perfection. Despite any failures or missteps, the dream will always be worth the risk.

Can you imagine our society if Thomas Edison had chosen not to dream instead of inventing the incandescent light bulb? What would have happened if Garrett Morgan, an African-American inventor from Ohio, had decided that his race and position in society disqualified him from dreaming about and inventing the gas mask and the gas light that became the traffic light? Are only a few born that have the fortitude to dream, create, and want more for their lives? No!

You are holding this book for a reason. Maybe you are curious about the process of figuring out your dreams. Perhaps you picked up this book hoping to understand why you long for more and don't know how to find your way. Maybe you have hidden dreams or a vision in your heart but you're afraid to step out or you doubt your ability to make them come true. Perhaps you have dreams and have been pursuing them for a while but find yourself discouraged, tired, disappointed, and wondering if the pursuit is really worth it. Maybe you used to dream for the future but life, adulthood, struggling, and obstacles have taught you that it is better not to dream than to dream a dream that never comes true.

Whatever your reasons for holding this book, you are not alone in your concerns, questions, or desires. You are simply looking for some answers and directions in taking the next steps to understanding why your life was created to be more. Your life is for greatness because your life is for a specific plan using your story and the dreams and vision placed in you.

During my younger years, I longed for a person, a book, a resource that would encourage me to follow the path less taken while helping me in my journey on that path. I desperately needed encouragement and direction in learning how to dream, pursue, and trust. Often, I felt alone and questioned if I should simply remain in the path that so many others seemed to settle for yet lived with frustration.

This is not a "how to" or four-step book but a journey in learning how to unleash your power. I would have desired this resource in seeking out my own dreams. This is not a shortcut to bringing your dreams to fruition. No one can shortcut a process that requires imagination, time, growth, and courage. Instead, this book is an encouragement guide to discovering the dreams and directions placed in you through understanding your story; I will walk with you as you prepare for your journey.

I must forewarn you, this book will not help you stay where you are or help you accept that your best attempt is good enough. This is for those who are ready to say "Yes!" to the invitation to Dream Madly, Pursue Wildly, and Trust Completely toward your best.

Also, this book is not to condemn anyone for the situations they are in or for their present condition due to a lack of dreaming. Nor is it written to demean, criticize, or judge any entity mentioned in these pages. The sole intent is to help you to remember your child-like hope and begin to dream again.

Before we can take our first step, we have to go back to the first question that stirred our imagination: "What did we want to be when we grew up?"

CHAPTER TWO

WHAT YOU WANTED TO BE WHEN YOU GREW UP

"Youth cannot know how age thinks and feels. But old men are guilty if they forget what it was to be young ... and I seem to have forgotten lately."

---- **Dumbledore in *Harry Potter and the Order of The Phoenix*
by J.K. Rowling**

Picture a little boy or girl sitting in their father's lap. The child is resting safe, totally relaxed within the father's strong arms. The legs of the child dangle over the father's legs like a lazy rag doll with arms stretched across the father's body. The head of the little boy or girl is cradled against the father's shoulder with wide-open eyes and a chattering mouth that gives no notice to the left-over chocolate cake frosting smearing their lips.

The father asks, "So what do you want to be when you grow up?" Immediately, the child's eyes brighten and he or she blurts out, "I wanna be an airplane pilot and fly higher than the trees!" Then the child continues to exclaim as the family dog runs into the room, "I wanna be a *vegetarian* so I can help animals to feel better." Before the father can open his mouth to say another word, the child yells, "Then, I wanna play football and be on television so I can wave to Mom and do a dance!"

The father holds his child tightly with joy admiring the lightness of heart and ability to take in so much without a care. He says to the child, "Which one of those things do you want to be when you grow up?" The child, in shock that the father would ask such a foolish question, replies, "All of them!"

"Really," the father responds. The little boy or girl simply says in great, childlike wisdom, "Why can't I do everything?"

The father smiles at the imagination and humor of that little mind. Before he can open his mouth to ask another question, the child continues to describe more dreams and hopes than a lifetime could contain. He dares not interrupt that moment because the child is doing something exciting and wonderful. That child is hoping. That child is believing in something greater than himself or herself. That child ... is dreaming.

Wow! What nerve! What gall! What risk for children to believe with conviction that their lives were not only meant to enjoy but to be fully enjoyed by others. They desire to experience and have all that is for them. Of course, a little child's mind does not comprehend all that. They just know, "I'm safe in my daddy's arms," "All that matters is now," and "I can dream and be anything and everything."

It is so easy to chuckle at the naïve ways of a child, and dismiss them as foolish or just children who don't know any better. We often believe life will correct their fantasy world and they will be better off once maturity sets in and they see things in a more realistic way.

Have we ever considered that regarding dreams, pursuits and trust, maybe it is the children, not the adults, who get it right? Have we ever considered that with each year of living, in our effort to be mature, perfect, and grown-up, we lose more and more of the natural beauty and ability to be childlike, and in so doing we limit our dreams, pursue more safely, and trust much less?

When a child is resting and dreaming in a father's arms they are not worrying about whether they will be as impressive as their competitors or whether anyone will read their books. The dreaming child is not fearful that he or she won't be good enough or talented enough to succeed. The child does not even care about what each step of the journey will look like or how long it will take. That free-spirited child only cares about now, feels a sense of safety and rest, and is able to do nothing but allow his or her mind to stretch to the farthest corners of imagination, without limitations.

That same dreaming child is not concerned that frosting has smeared his or her face or slobber is running down. Man, that kid is just chilling out and relaxing knowing that Daddy has it handled; they are in the moment and are free to explore the possibilities.

That freedom to dream, create, and imagine does not sound foolish or naïve to me at all. Actually, that way of dreaming describes how we are all to dream.

How much would our lives change if we began to relive the dreams we had as a child and experienced the freedom of drawing from a clean slate of imagination toward possibilities, potential, and purpose? Regardless of where we are now or how many dreams we have left by the wayside, there was a time when dreams were easy to create and possibilities were endless.

BORN TO DREAM

Babies and young children move boldly. They are creative, curious pursuers. They appear unafraid unless they catch the fearful glance of an adult. They are dreamers.

Dr. Charles P. Pollak, director of the Center for Sleep Medicine at New York-Presbyterian/Weill Cornell Medical Center, states, "At 24-30 weeks gestational age the unborn baby dreams at 100 percent." He further states, "Their dreams are connected with the passionate drive to survive, to relate, to learn, and grow." [1]

Babies and young children take in life in a way we often take for granted as adults. Something is wired into a baby that seems to fade as we face life and begin to see the world through older, safer, adult eyes.

An interesting phenomenon takes place when we are babies and young children that changes as we grow older. Babies and young children engage in something called abdominal breathing. Every time they breathe or take in air, the diaphragm, which is the main muscle the body uses for breathing, stretches downward and allows their lungs to fill to full capacity. When they breathe out or release the air, the diaphragm contracts upward and decreases lung volume. With abdominal breathing, the lungs expand to two times the volume because they are fully engaged.

Babies, young children, and even animals breathe abdominally, which is the correct way to breathe. Next time you are close to your cat or dog or any animal in the wild, watch it at rest. You will notice when it inhales, its abdomen expands outward, and when it exhales, its abdomen contracts inward to expel the air in the lungs.

Babies, young children, and animals seem instinctively to know how to rest their bodies as well as their minds fully. I have often envied my two cats, Cole and Conner, while they are sleeping. Within moments, they will find a comfortable area under the pillows of my bed or on top of their carpeted cat penthouse to fall asleep. Conner will curl up on his side with his paw over his head while Cole prefers her "I think I am a dog so I'm going to sleep on my back with four paws in the air" position. They dream, they trust, and they rest.

Outside an occasional REM dream, like the baby and young child, the cats exist in a world of rest and the "now" without stress, fear, worry, self-doubt, or comparison. Day after day, we watch our pets, babies and young children sleep and breathe calmly and perfectly without a care in the world.

Unlike our first years, as we grow older, gradually we become upper-chest breathers who rely on the muscles of the chest and shoulders to breathe. Our improper breathing over time can increase our bodies' stress response and possibly cause other stress-related conditions. Amazingly, from our first breath, something in us cries for more and breathes in as if we instinctively know a reserve will be needed for a future that will require a great deal.

Young children's minds run toward possibilities and freedom without regard to something as insignificant as rules or reality. They see the glass half-full and look at a future based on their desires and joys instead of others' views or opinions. They are free and wild and untamed because they dream for more.

DREAMING LIKE A CHILD

When was the last time you allowed yourself to dream like a child? When was the last time you wondered what you wanted to be when you grew up? When was the last time you allowed yourself to escape from the believed boundaries, limitations, situations, and stresses in your life long enough to ask, "What if?" When was the last time you allowed yourself to dream a dream big enough to fail?

Just for one moment, close your eyes and try to remember that very first dream you held close that you knew with all your heart would one day happen. Can you remember? Does it bring a slight smile to your face?

Now remember the freedom and innocence of that dream. Nothing was too big or too silly. It did not matter that the dream changed with each new sight, experience, or adventure of the day. It was your dream and it was your stake and claim to the future. All you knew or cared about was one day when you grew up you were going to be …

What You Wanted To Be When You Grew Up

I remember having dreams as a little girl that gave great insight regarding the people, places, and things that influenced my life the most. When I was a little girl, I stayed with my grandparents most of the time while my parents worked and my brother and sisters went to school.

My grandmother was incredible. I saw the love she had for being a mother, wife, and homemaker. During her time, society viewed a homemaker as a valuable contributor, and it was something I longed to become. I dreamed of growing up, marrying the strong and tall man of my dreams, and having a family with a boy named Conner, a girl named Callie, and a cat.

Life situations, different roads, and different choices never brought that particular childhood dream into reality (except for the cat). For some, that fact would prove the belief it is better not to dream than to dream and fail. However, it proves quite the opposite.

Without the dreams of my childhood, I would have missed some of the best years of my life. My journey helped me discover my childhood dreams were not my deepest desires but simply great passions. My dreams gave hope to the passions of my heart despite not knowing the path. Those dreams offered me glimpses of hope for a future that had not happened yet in the midst of loneliness, fear and the troubled world I knew as a child. My childhood dream in my grandparents' house far from failed.

No matter how wonderful our childhoods were or how painful, in some part, there was a secret place to dream and to wonder about a world, a place, and a time outside of our present circumstance. In a very loving way, we have been equipped with an automatic "escape to hope" button in the form of our dreams.

When we were sad and needed a place to propel us into the future, we could push our dream button to imagine the events of a faraway place. When we were in the midst of struggle and felt like giving up in the middle of our journey, we could also hit that button as a reminder of what we were toiling and pressing forward to attain.

We were born to dream, to yearn for more than the ordinary day-to-day provides. We feel that yearning each time we hear a story of someone accomplishing their own dreams or achieving great heights. We love to read and watch biographies of people's lives and the harrowing escapes, sacrifices, and challenges they went through. Their stories stir up the dreams in us.

We realize we have been created to dream every time we feel that unsatisfied knot of discontentment in our stomachs that cries out, "There has got to be more to my life!" That knot is a confirmation that we have been wired to dream for a time that has not yet occurred.

Not only were we born to dream for the future, but we also were born to dream dreams that are big enough to fail, dreams that are so big and impossible only a miracle would bring them to pass. In short, we were born to Dream Madly, Pursue Wildly, and Trust Completely.

ACTING LIKE AN ADULT

Although my grandparents were my foundation in learning to dream, as time moved on, that foundation was not strong enough to prevent my wonderful world of dreaming from crashing down. Unfortunately, like most of us, the innocence of my childhood imagination was crushed and lost as I learned to be "more adult" and journey through the reality of life. I quickly learned that dreams are for dreamers and are made to be put on the shelf of "maybes, tomorrows, one days, and I used tos."

Many struggles, obstacles, and dream stealers have come into my life. I found out dreaming for a future, moving toward visions, and finding the courage to take another step in spite of discouragement and exhaustion are incredible feats that take more than simple positive thinking to accomplish.

By now, you might be asking, "If I was born to Dream Madly, Pursue Wildly, and Trust Completely, why am I having so much difficulty doing it?" The answer is simple. Over time, many of us were subtly taught and masterfully learned how to stop dreaming, pursuing and trusting.

Our lack of dreaming is no longer a prejudice we can place in the laps of the unfortunate, misplaced, and underprivileged. Our society has settled in a deep, hollow place. It is a place where, I believe, we shall surely perish into an accepting world of being hopeless should we continue in our present path. The ability and the joyful freedom to dream have left us to wonder if there is any hope for the future.

Some learned by watching the struggles of their parents or a single parent in providing for the family. Dreams did not put food on the table, so life turned in a more practical direction. Over time, dreams were placed on the shelf and exchanged for ten-hour workdays, savings accounts, an easier life, and subdued discontentment.

Some learned early by being told their dreams had no value and hope was an extravagance only other children could afford. They learned through abuse, isolation, bullying, neglect, name-calling, shame, and guilt that neither they nor their dreams mattered. They learned early to trade hopes and dreams for control, walls of safety, distrust, fear, and lies that their potential was lost.

I remember one of my first lessons in holding back dreams. My older sister teased me after catching me practicing a song in the bathroom. I was a little girl pretending to sing my show-stopping song in front of a crowded room. I had my pencil microphone in one hand and my other hand raised up to express the movement of the song. As I hit the high note of the song, my sister busted in to laugh at me and shout, "You sound horrible! You're not good enough to be a singer." I was heartbroken and ran in shame to my bedroom.

As tears rolled down my face, my thoughts turned immediately to an audience laughing and pointing at me on stage because I sang a bad note. I wondered if my sister knew more than I did and began to convince myself that I was foolish to believe in my talent. It took only minutes for me to doubt myself for having such a dream.

Some have learned to hold back their dreams because of words said or actions done to them similar to my sister's words. Others learned simply through the journey of growing older and living life. The daily news, war, economic crisis, rejection, relationships, work, marriage, failed plans, lack of control, children, health, in-laws, and the day-to-day of life slowly drained the excitement of dreams away and left an explanation of obligations, limitations, and obstacles in its place.

Perhaps if we could lock out the unfairness of life and people we could dream freely like a child forever. However, people will always be around us and life will remain unfair. Time passes and inevitably, someone will say something to us or an event will happen to cause us to doubt forever having such a dream. Unless we challenge that doubt, it will become a fear. The fear eventually moves to a distraction. The distraction turns into an occasional thought then eventually, we will place it on the shelf with other "dreams we will get around to someday."

Unfortunately, most times our dreams, unlike the sun, turn and move away. People criticize, mistakes happen, feelings are hurt, life changes, we grow older and our dreams move away in the process. The hopeful child who once dreamed freely of possibilities with an overflowing imagination slowly learns to be realistic and practical and begins to act like an adult.

Time, life, and growing older changed not our ability, but our willingness to dream, pursue, and trust. The wisdom and freedom we once held in our childhood somehow got lost once we started acting like adults. Unconsciously, we grew older yet left the wonders of being childlike behind.

Our childlike imagination that only knew the limitations of our creativity learned to color within the lines of what we believed we could control with an earnest effort. Instead of allowing our imagination to lead us to take risks, try new things, make discoveries, and walk unknown paths, it became easier to limit our imagination to fit what was safe, comfortable, and unchallenging.

Self-doubt, dream stealers, rejection, and the distorted belief that our feelings and scars were a reflection of our future influenced the beauty of being in the "now" and invited comparison to others' dreams.

We did not try to stop dreaming, pursuing, or trusting. However, as we grew older and experienced living, life taught us that dreaming was an option instead of a necessity for living. Dreaming seemed to be something that "certain people" did or were just stories we read or viewed at the movie theatres.

To some, dreaming was a negative action relegated to the fickle, "head in the clouds," non-Christian-like, slightly crazy person who dreamed instead of being "practical." The idea of dreaming for something without immediate results was ludicrous.

Dreaming Madly is risky, life changing, thrilling, imaginative, joyful, and more. However, the thing it is not is ludicrous. Dreaming Madly is not about making a wish and hoping it comes true. It is a practice, which becomes a habit, which turns into a way of life. It is a return to seeing yourself and the world around you through childlike wonder with adult wisdom and experience.

Often people, situations, and life influence our dreams instead of our dreams impacting the people, places, and things of our life. Our dreams are meant to be like a constant sun glowing in the distance as we move around and around on our journey through life. Sometimes the path is bright and clear and our life is easily moving forward. Other times, darkness, pain, hardships, struggles, and unexpected situations enter our life and nothing makes sense as we take each next step. Still dreams remain, reminding us that we still have a future to grab hold of and possibilities to conquer.

Conquering those possibilities and grabbing hold of that future requires a journey. It is a journey of pursuit, which will take preparation and strength. The difficulty for some will stem from beliefs and fears. It is a journey of trust, which will take courage. The difficulty for others will stem from experiences and history in trusting. The first part of the journey is learning how to dream again. For most, it is very difficult and is often the path less taken.

CHAPTER TWO

TO DREAM MADLY:
THE PATH LESS TAKEN

"The center of every man's existence is a dream."

---- **G. K. Chesterton, in** *Twelve Types* **(1903), "Sir Walter Scott"**

In 2010, I released a book called *Damaged Goods: Learning to Dream Again* about the sexual and physical abuse of my past and my journey of learning how to dream again in the face of hopelessness. In the process of writing, I discovered many people, regardless of their experiences, lost their dreams while walking out their lives.

After the book's release, I received numerous emails and letters from those who lost dreams, longed to begin to dream but were afraid, and those who didn't know how to start dreaming. I was overwhelmed and intrigued. I wanted to find out more and began researching why dreaming, hoping, and moving toward potential and possibilities seemed to be so out of reach.

In the summer of 2010, I created a true-or-false, general statement survey to evaluate beliefs, perceptions, and desires regarding dreams and people's lives. The statements reflected overall thoughts and anonymous discussions from my past counselling clients and additional suggestions from colleagues who are therapists.

According to the results of the survey, we left dreams and hopes at the doorstep of our youth. Of the 2,034 respondents, the majority believed dreams were a luxury they could not afford because of the situations they faced and the beliefs they held.

The survey uncovered a wealth of information and beliefs regarding why we still long to dream for more but don't because of obstacles, believed or real, that stand in the way. As we continue to discover our way back to the childlike freedom to dream again, more results from the survey and answers to how to dream, pursue and trust will be uncovered.

Although the survey revealed the many reasons and beliefs we have for not dreaming, it is more important to understand the reasons why it is vital to dream and what it means to Dream Madly.

First, the events and stories of our life are meant to impact others. While our dreams do not always reveal our purpose or calling, they help to bridge and answer the passions in our life that come out of our story and experiences.

Second, despite obstacles and difficulties, our life is meant to be more than a journey of enduring, suffering, living, and settling for ordinary. Our dreams expose the desires of our heart and the hopes that we long for in the midst of living. Dreams take us out of the mundane and prompt us into possibilities.

Third, it is vital to dream simply because a life without movement or direction toward something is easily distracted, depressed, discontented and driven to hopelessness. A dream or vision will never take place if it is not lived out.

Fourth, we are born to dream and to pursue those dreams. People usually do not stop dreaming because their lives are fulfilled. They usually stop dreaming because of an obstacle, negative situation, misguided belief, or loss that makes the ability to dream foreign.

The final reason it is vital to dream is because our future and our impact on others' lives are greater and more important than any fear, doubt or desire for safety.

We are never too young or too old to dream. We are never too dumb, poverty-stricken, sickly, abused, jacked up, messed up, or even fed up to dream. Our present situations can never limit our dreams. Our past trauma, mistakes or regrets can never discourage or disqualify us from our dreams. Our dream stealers, naysayers, heart breakers, or hope takers can never keep us from our dreams. The only one who can thwart us from our dreams ... is us.

What would happen if we believed that no idea was too silly or out of bounds? That no thought was overrated or egotistical? That no dream or desire was too big or too dangerous to come true? That limitations of age, gender, education, background or even handicap were not considerations or seen as obstacles in the way of the dream? That the world was a place of possibilities and a distant voice was calling out, "Why not?" What if all we knew and believed was that we're safe and acceptable and that our desires and dreams, regardless of the journey, were in reach? What if we had the audacity to believe the future held a hope, a promise of some kind, and we would be a part of it?

If we believed that way, we would be doing what we were born to do. We have a better understanding of why it is vital to dream, but what does it mean to Dream Madly?

WHAT DOES IT MEAN TO DREAM MADLY?

Dreaming Madly is just what the words say. It is exploring and allowing ourselves to dream about what we are to do and be without regard to the obstacles or limitations that prevent us from dreaming as we used to before life taught us to grow up and settle for what is in front of us. It is allowing ourselves to return to a place of childlike vulnerability, possibility, hope, risk, and freedom to see our potential and greatness through less battle-scarred eyes toward a life that matters.

To Dream Madly means taking a risk to believe against what we might think about ourselves. It means taking a risk to dismiss what others have said, the past, and the current circumstances long enough to close our eyes and ask, "What if?"

Dreaming Madly is not positive thinking; once something bad or disappointing happens, the dream leaves also. Dreaming Madly is not settling for what we are able to do, because anyone of simple means and intelligence can accomplish a task. Dreaming Madly is not about doing something because someone thinks we should or wants us to do something. If the dream is not ours, it is certainly not worth the journey it will take to pursue it well.

Dreaming Madly stirs our imagination, excitement, adventure, and joy. However, we often we confuse the simple and wondrous ability to imagine for the future with the act of working out the details and seeing it through to its fruition. They are not the same. Dreaming has little or nothing to do with work, performance, goals, doing, planning, or seeing things through. That confusion and frustration alone often makes the journey of Dreaming Madly a path less taken.

Sometimes, we stop dreaming before we begin because of our lack of understanding of what dreaming is and is not. Words like *dreams, night dreams, visions, goals,* and *purpose* become clouded in our search to understand the true meaning.

A DREAM IS NOT THE SAME AS A VISION

Often, we confuse dreams with visions. Both can deal with a future time and place, but they are not the same. If a dream is a canvas then vision is the art. According to the Merriam-Webster Dictionary, there are three definitions of a vision. The first is the *"Mode or power of seeing or conceiving."* The second is *"A thought, concept, or object formed by the imagination."*

The definition we are focusing on is the third definition, which is *"An experience in which a personage, thing, or event appears vividly or credibly to the mind, although not actually present, often under the influence of a divine or other agency."* [1]

A vision is something given to the receiver and can offer foresight or insight about the future or a change. Visions cause us to see beyond the natural realm. A person is the observer in a vision and there is no interaction.

Unlike a vision, a dream is created by the receiver and is experienced in the natural realm. There are two definitions of dreaming according to the Merriam-Webster Dictionary. First, a dream is *"A series of images, ideas, emotions, and sensations occurring involuntarily in the mind during certain stages of sleep."* The definition of dreaming we are focusing on is the second: *"A wild fancy or hope; a condition or achievement that is longed for; an aspiration."* 2

Unlike a vision, a dream causes us to long for more and is something we receive and participate in. In a dream, a person usually interacts with the scene in some way.

Both visions and dreams move us to look beyond what we see as ordinary, possible, and easily obtainable. Whether received from another as a vision or self-created as a dream, it propels us toward a future and a hope that has not happened yet.

A DREAM IS NOT THE SAME AS A GOAL

There is a saying that goes, "A dream without a plan is simply a fantasy." That saying is correct. A plan and a goal are both needed to move a dream to its fruition, but they are not the same.

Dreams are the unlimited imaginary journey while a goal is limited and has a realistic point of destination. A person can dream through an entire lifetime without ever moving forward or stepping out on the dream. Like the growing imagination of a child, dreams are not attached to a time limit. We could wait the rest of our lives to see a dream turn into reality. We can also have a goal without giving much thought to dreaming. Our dreams are the desired end product and hope while our goals are the means to achieve dreams.

Goals are conscious decisions for plans or intentions we have for the future. Our goals can be long term, such as a plan to go back to school to earn a higher degree or GED. Our goals can also be short term, such as making plans to see a movie or go shopping with a friend in the afternoon.

Our goals show an act of commitment while our dreams do not. In short, a dream is something we hope and desire will take place without any work or movement on our part. A goal is something we decide to do and then set up a plan of action to accomplish.

A SLEEPING DREAM IS NOT THE SAME AS A DREAM AWAKE

Understanding the difference between a dream while we are asleep and a dream while we are awake is tricky. Both can look to the future, cling to a hope, or bring great excitement and longing. However, the major distinction between the two is control.

When we sleep, we experience two major states that consist of four stages of sleep. Our body cycles between non-REM and REM sleep. *"Typically, people begin the sleep cycle with a period of non-REM (non Rapid Eye Movement) sleep followed by a very short period of REM sleep. Dreams generally occur in the REM stage of sleep."* [3]

In our first stage of sleep, which lasts approximately five to ten minutes, our eyes are closed but we can be awakened without difficulty.

Next, we enter a second stage of sleep where our heart rate slows and our temperature decreases in preparation for deeper sleep. We enter deep sleep in the third and fourth stages. If we are aroused during those stages, we will often feel disoriented. Intense dreaming occurs during REM sleep due to heightened brain activity, but paralysis occurs simultaneously in the major voluntary muscle groups. In that stage, we are paralyzed from the neck down, our eye movements are jerky and rapid, our heart rate fluctuates, and our breathing changes.

Interestingly, REM sleep is highest while we are babies and during early childhood. During adolescence and young adulthood, REM sleep declines. Babies sleep in the REM stage about fifty percent of the time while adults only spend about twenty percent in REM sleep.

Sleeping dreams not only help the body to repair and regenerate tissues, build bone and muscle, and appear to strengthen the immune system, but they have occurred at times to offer a warning or prophecy of something in the present or future, according to the Bible.

In the Old Testament and some of the New Testament, people were given a warning, prophecy, or encouragement (which was not as common) through their dreams while asleep.

Joseph, the son of Jacob, had a dream regarding his future and the position he would hold. Another Joseph, the husband of Mary, received a dream in which he was told not to fear taking Mary as his wife because the Holy Spirit conceived her child, Jesus. Abimelech had a dream regarding Abraham's wife, Sarah, and was forewarned not to come near her. Jacob had a dream that his descendants would be like the dust of the earth and would spread out to the west, to the east, to the north, and to the south.

In the case of sleeping dreams, the body responds outside of our control. Dreams may certainly be a reflection of something or someone in our daily life and potential reality. However, they generally do not offer indicators of our purpose in life, nor can we control them according to how we desire to move forward toward a life that matters. Surprisingly, our dreams while awake do have those qualities.

Dreams are extensions of our purpose, give imagination to our goals or visions, and operate differently than when we are asleep.

Now that we have a definition of dreaming, it is time to begin to dream again. We will need to gather tools and set landmarks for the journey ahead. Our landmark is someone who was an example of the ultimate dreamer. His name was Jack Kavanagh.

CHAPTER FOUR

BEGINNING TO DREAM AGAIN
"Where [there is] no vision, the people perish."

---- **Proverbs 29:18***(KJV)*

People need something to move them toward hope and push them toward the future. One obstacle that often prevents us from stepping out on our dreams and visions is the belief that we simply don't have visions or dreams. We witness this daily in the current generation that is trained to focus on present gain instead of waiting, planning, hoping, and holding off for something greater.

However, the parents and grandparents of the current generation are also falling into the hopeless trap of "I don't have any dreams." Like everything, dreams are a choice but they will always be worth the risk and the journey.

A while ago, I had a conversation with a buddy of mine, Jim Kavanagh. We discussed new dreams he was pursuing and his deep love for his wife. In the midst of the conversation, Jim mentioned his father and told me of the great influence his father had on the family, community, and those around him before he passed.

I was blown away as Jim described the obstacles his father endured and the courage he offered in spite of his defeats. I was humbled to the point of tears of hearing about a man who exemplified the meaning of being a dreamer. He was truly a remarkable man who, despite obstacles, advanced years, responsibilities, and more, Dreamed Madly, Pursued Wildly, and Trusted Completely.

I asked Jim if he would be willing to share the story of his remarkable dad in my book. He did. Here is the story of Jack Kavanagh, a dad, a friend, a simple man, and a dreamer.

"My dad, Jack Kavanagh, never went hunting in his life, but he knew how to stay on the trail of an elusive dream.

While still a student at the University of Detroit, Jack fell in love with the study of philosophy and decided to make a career of it. He set his sights on becoming a professor. However, right about that time Japan set its sights on Pearl Harbor. He enlisted in the Navy and married his high school sweetheart, Catherine "Honey" Boyle, in the spring of 1942. A baby was on the way by the time he shipped out to the South Pacific.

Jack served as the communications officer aboard the destroyer USS Patterson throughout the conflict. Thanks to occasional leaves and an accident that put the Patterson in dry dock for a few months, he was welcomed home after the war by Honey and three babies who looked just like him – except that they had more hair.

With the war concluded, Jack took advantage of the GI Bill to return to Detroit and earn his master's degree. He was unable to secure a teaching position, but a job writing stories for Ward's Automotive Reports helped pay the bills and feed the babies, who were joined by a fourth in 1948.

As more children continued to arrive (hey, my parents were Irish Catholics; this is how it went back then), my dad needed a better-paying job. He landed a position with the Michigan Department of Commerce, which soon necessitated a move to the capital, Lansing. *His job was to "sell Michigan," persuading industrial companies to build factories, warehouses and distribution centers in the state. He was good at it. However, it wasn't his dream job.*

Jack and Honey's 11th and final child arrived in March 1960. (That would be me.) The eldest, Cathy, was getting ready to start college. With 11 children enrolled in parochial schools or college, taking music lessons, playing sports and insisting on wearing clothes and eating every single day, money was as tight as it could be. *My older siblings have described seeing Dad turn our big dining room table into a bill-paying triage center: He had to decide which ones he could ignore for a while, which he could get away with making a token payment on, and which had to be paid right now.*

It's a testimony to both of my parents that even though we never had a lot of money, we never felt deprived.

Jack's work sometimes took him away from home for three to five days at a time, intervals that showed just how tall my 4-foot-11-inch mother stood as a leader and organizer. Everyone still in the household, from the oldest to the youngest, had chores and responsibilities, including looking after one another. It worked.

Other than when he was on those business trips, my dad was home with the family for dinner at that big table every night. He was a lector at the church and a member of the parish council and school board. He and my mother read to us, talked with us and listened to us. They took us to church, they taught us how to study, they attended our games and track meets and school plays. They delighted in us, they disciplined us, and they demonstrated what love is for us.

By the time I was 15, most of my siblings had been married or otherwise moved out, so there was more elbowroom in the house and more breathing room in the budget. The time was ripe for Jack Kavanagh's long-dormant dream to start stirring again.

Jack started taking night classes at nearby Michigan State University. Honey, even after a long day of housework in a long life of housework, diligently banged out his papers on an electric typewriter on the dining room table. Together they pushed the dream forward. There were no online classes then, no podcasts of lectures, no looking things up on the internet. Students had to go to classes, take notes, and put in the time to read and do research at the library.

In the spring of 1979, my mother threw a huge party for my father in a ballroom on the MSU campus. The occasion comprised four celebrations: Jack and Honey's 37th wedding anniversary, Jack's 59th birthday, the conferral of Jack's Ph.D. in philosophy – he'd written his dissertation on business ethics – and his retirement after 30 years of service to the state.

He was just getting started.

Jack and Honey packed up and moved east, where he joined the faculty of the University of Delaware's Center for the Study of Values. After several years they returned to Michigan, where Jack taught at small colleges and fought off colon cancer before moving on to yet another career: writing brief sermons to be used by Catholic priests during weekday Masses. He did that well into his 70s.

After my mother suffered a heart attack, my dad took over the cooking duties for good. They did everything as partners, including heading home to heaven just 19 days apart.

Arm-in-arm with Honey, Jack never let go of his dream despite every obstacle, encumbrance, detour, and delay. There were never excuses, only perseverance, belief, and determination.

That is how a dream stays alive."
~ *Jim Kavanagh*

Jack Kavanagh was a dreamer and an example of someone who Dreamed Madly. He was able to recapture an imagination and a hope for a time that had not happened yet. He caught on to the understanding that Dreaming Madly involves allowing oneself to return to a place of innocent dreaming, safety and full imagination that is comparable to being held in a father's arms.

How do we really begin to dream again? How do we start that first baby step to crowd out the worries and realities of being a limited adult and return to that place of limitless imagination and dreaming? How do we begin allowing ourselves to dream about what we are meant to do and be without regard to the obstacles or limitations?

Dreaming starts by preparing the setting and gathering the necessary tools for the journey. It involves returning to a place and a setting where we allowed ourselves the freedom to dream and imagine without limitations. In order to recall that place of rest we need to understand the dream stealers that will creep into our path to discourage, distract, detain, and deter us before we get started.

The five major dream stealers are fear, the past, feelings, people, and performance. During the course of understanding each dream stealer, we will be working on an exercise. The purpose of the exercise is to connect possible sources and messages we received to the dream stealers that get in the way of Dreaming Madly, Pursuing Wildly, and Trusting Completely in our lives.

CHAPTER FIVE

DREAM STEALER #1- FEAR

"Courage is not the lack of fear but the ability to face it."

---- Lt. John B. Putnam Jr. (1921-1944)

A few years ago, I was part of a group of church volunteers helping with a community service project. The church coordinated with some of the local organizations and businesses to seek out areas and clients that needed assistance on a designated Saturday.

Some of the volunteers worked in homes in the neighborhood painting, cleaning, doing chores, and tidying lawns. Others volunteered to help at schools, shelters, and local businesses to clean offices, make light repairs, and build things.

The daughter of a homeowner asked my group to come to her house to clean as part of the housing project. The mother, embarrassed by the roach infestation and condition of her home, only relented after her daughter's daily pleading for help.

When I entered the house, I was immediately struck by a disturbing situation. It was not the condition or unclean state of the house. Unlike cooking, gardening, laundry or any other domesticated duty, I love to clean and merely saw it as a challenge. It was not even the insect infestation. While I do believe there is no need for the existence of a small multi-legged critter unless it is an official pet belonging in the house, I saw roaches before and was not overwhelmed.

The situation I was greatly disturbed about was the level of hopelessness and contentment of despair that signalled that the days of dreaming for something more had long left that home. I looked into the eyes of a mother who admittedly gave up dreaming years ago and had settled into a life of cable television, cell phones, junk food, and the presence of a man who seemingly cared little for her. I looked into the eyes of a six-year-old boy who had no clue what an ocean was until I described the blues and greens and the still sands of a beach while sliding water down his face.

My greatest sadness came from the dead eyes looking at me from the seventeen-year-old daughter, pregnant with her second child, who could give me no answer to my question about her dreams and plans. I asked her the same question I asked others daily: "In five years, what do you dream for yourself?" She replied, "I'm afraid to dream."

My heart sank. I pressed further to ask why she was so afraid to dream. That young woman could not conceive of travelling overseas, being a doctor, curing a disease or even something as hopeful as graduating from school and having a nice home of her own because she was frightened to hope for more than she knew. We talked as I continued to sweep the floor of the tiny room she shared with her first child's crib. We laughed, we cried, we talked more about dreams and goals, and then we cleaned together.

When I left the home of that young woman, she felt encouraged, inspired, and even made plans to move in a new direction. Although I gave her my number to call for help, I never heard from her again. I truly hope she stuck to her plan to move forward.

Often we categorize that young woman as merely a tragic victim of her circumstance, sit back, and say, "What a shame!" However, the reality is that the same deadness and lack of dreaming for the future pervades our entire society from the highest-paid politician and celebrity to the pastor of thousands, the homemaker, the man living in a shelter and the everyday working stiff. The first dream stealer is the greatest and most powerful of all. It is fear.

WHAT IS FEAR?

A four-letter word has killed and put more people behind bars than guns. It has brought down more marriages, led to more suicides, and ruined more political careers than any winning candidate's votes in history. It has caused more losses, bailouts, buyouts, greed, prophecies, predictions, name-calling, blame switching, finger pointing, and downright lying than the greasiest hands on Wall Street.

This four-letter word has cut off more potential, closed the door to more possibilities, and clamped shut down more great plans, inventions, ideas, and creativity than one could ever imagine. That same four-letter word daily steals away courage to dream for more toward a life that matters.

One of the greatest dream stealers that prevent us from stepping out on our dreams and visions is fear. Fear stops us in our tracks. Although fear can be our friend that warns us of impending danger, more often it is an enemy that attacks through our assumptions, beliefs, thoughts, and of course, the unknown road ahead. It tells us not to move forward without evidence, that danger truly exists or will overtake us. It gives us that queasy feeling that something is not right or is strange.

What is fear? *"Fear is the anxiety or unpleasant concern we have in anticipation of something we perceive as danger or discomfort. It is anything we perceive as an assault to our comfort, safety, or control."* 1   Fear-motivated thoughts are all about "I can't," "I'm not able," and "I'm not good enough." While we certainly have fears and phobias of the things, people, or situations in our path, more often we fear the negative feeling we will experience because of that thing, person, or situation in our path.

For example, let's say a woman named Mary wants to write a book about her life but she is fearful that people won't like it and others will be angry that she told secrets that happened in the past. Mary is not afraid of writing the book, telling her story or even the people who will read the book. Her fear is the possible rejection, disappointment, and feeling of failure she will experience by others if she moves forward in writing the book.

Our fears stem from our anticipation of something happening. We anticipate negative and terrible things that might happen or things we have heard about, seen through the media, or read. Fear makes us think that something bad or negative will take place, when the truth is we don't know what is going to happen. Most of us have not been insulted or booed in front of a stage audience, but that does not stop us from going into a panic if we are called to give a lecture in front of thousands.

Fear is always designed to offer a false sense of safety and comfort. It gives the impression that if we stay away from whatever that perceived fear is, then we will be all right, safe and pain-free. The catch is that in that false safety there is also limitation, discontentment, and limited growth. Fear has no wisdom and fear has no truth.

Often we fear not because of the reality of a situation but because of our anticipation of what could happen in that situation. In short, our fears cry aloud that we are not in control of something, and that is not pleasant at all.

Why do we fear? Part of the answer is that we have inherent fears placed in us for survival purposes. Without being taught, our stomachs begin to feel queasy and our heart beats fast when we are on the edge of a cliff or facing a roaring lion. Our bodies alert us to clear and present danger that we should flee from or resist.

We also fear because of conditioning and our environment. Michael Lewis, director of the Institute for the Study of Child Development at Robert Wood Johnson Medical School in New Brunswick, New Jersey, states, *"We learn to become fearful* *through experience with the fear event, or learning from those people around us like our parents, our siblings, and our colleagues."*2

Fear conditioning is why some people fear new adventures or certain types of dogs while others embrace adventures and run to dogs as if each were their personal pet. It is why some fear dreaming, hoping, or trusting for a life that truly matters and others boldly go where others dare to travel.

In other words, we learn to fear through the experiences and events that shape our lives. We don't wake up at age 28 or 50 and suddenly become fearful of asking for help or sharing an imperfection in our lives. We learn through time and experience to fear.

We learn fear from being told that we will be hurt or fail if we try a certain act or take a chance in doing something. We learn to fear by being rejected by someone and feeling the pain of embarrassment and shame and decide we will do whatever is necessary to prevent that type of pain again. We learn to fear after believing years' worth of lies that tell us our past mistakes and harms have disqualified us from doing great things and achieving new heights.

THE POWER OF FEAR

We fear many things, and we always hate what we fear. While painful, sometimes it is easier and safer to believe we will fail than to believe we will succeed. We fear being alone, being hurt by others, being abandoned, and the feeling of not being lovable. We fear failure, rejection, making mistakes, not being good at something, having to depend on someone, showing our imperfections, and the feeling of not being worthwhile.

We fear taking risks, walking into the unknown, taking chances, and the possibility we will not have control. We fear not fitting into a certain group, being different, not agreeing with others, and the feeling of not being acceptable.

We also fear dreaming, hoping, sharing our dreams, taking risks, and wanting more because in the back of our minds we hear the whisper, "What you long for will never happen, at least not for you." We anticipate our inabilities, failures, and disqualifications before making a first step in reality.

All too often, the conditioning we receive is based on false beliefs and negative circumstances that leave a message that something is lacking in us and to hope for anything but the easily obtainable will always be out of reach.

Neale Donald Walsch coined the acronym FEAR as **F**alse **E**vidence **A**ppearing **R**eal. I would like to coin the acronym for Fear as **F**ailure **E**qually **A**pplied to **R**eality because we often create that as fear's definition.

More than being false evidence, fear to a great many people equals failure, mistakes, and lack of success. Our fear comes from the assumption that something we will do or a dream or action we will take for the future will result in a failure and mistake. That fear of failure becomes a reality we apply to our lives and avoid it at all costs. For some, dreaming is a risk of failure that is too big to take. That is the power of fear. That is failure equally applied to reality.

THE TRUTH ABOUT FEAR

Fear has absolutely no power outside of what we give it. Although our fears feel overwhelming and real, the truth is most fears regarding the future and the unknown are based on our imagination, not fact. As long as we believe our fears are real, we will remain immobilized and our fears will control us. If we view fear for what it is, a simple indicator of something else going on in our lives, we can overcome and take back its power. The challenge is difficult but possible.

I remember a time when I had to face my great fear in returning home to Ohio after living in my beloved Nashville for years.

I was enjoying a gorgeous spring day of reading and relaxing under a tree at the Parthenon when the thought of going home entered my mind. I quickly threw out the idea as crazy and continued reading my book and enjoying the comfort of my new hometown.

I moved through the next few days by working at the radio station overnights, counselling clients, and speaking around town during the day. Despite my work distractions, I could not shake my crazy thoughts about needing to go home. I didn't understand why I felt a strange leading to go back home, but I knew it was something I was supposed to do. Each day the thought was becoming louder in my head. Unfortunately, I was not interested in going back home for any reason.

I was afraid to go back to Ohio. To me, home represented a world of pain, conflict, misconceptions, and people who, I believed, only saw me through the eyes of my damage and past. I was afraid I would experience the great hurt and rejection I felt in the past. I feared seeing my mother who did not understand my life's work and viewed me as weak because I broke the silence about the abuse that lingered in our home for years. Returning to a place like that made no sense to me.

I remember telling God that if he wanted me to go back to Ohio, back to that place of pain and judgment, he was going to have to personally come down and get me because I was not going!

After a month and a half of losing my apartment, doors closing at every turn, failed attempts to find a place to rent, and experiencing the daily guilt that I was running from doing what I knew to do despite my great fear, I decided it was time to go back home.

My drive back to Ohio was long and lonely. I was returning with a belief that I was to go home and I was going to bring disruption to my relationships. So much had happened since

I lived in Ohio. Although I was still in the process of healing and growing up, I was a different person than when I left years ago.

During my initial months in Ohio, I found difficulty in people accepting a Charlotte who was then emotional, tender, desired relationship, and challenged words and statements people said. Understandably, people still perceived me as distant, unapproachable, and uncaring. My requests to move to a deeper level of relationship were met with surprise, suspicion, and difficulty in viewing me in any way other than from the past.

I also began to see a further disruption in the relationship between my mother and me. Time had passed and we had become different people. I had firm boundaries and a perspective that came from viewing the dynamics of my family as an outsider. My mother had become a Christian and was trying to regain a family relationship that had long disappeared. Often when we met, we were like two strangers in a room not knowing what to say or do with each other. I was in her company on some occasions when she was less demanding in her conversations and understood my boundaries regarding honesty and family gossip. During other occasions, I would experience the mother of my youth using words of guilt, shame, accusations, and claims of reparations she felt I owed her for years of mothering me.

Unlike the days of my youth, her words no longer held power over me. Time had passed and I was no longer a little girl searching for love, acceptance, and worth through her value or view of me. A boundary was set and over the next two years, a theme of disruption took place with my mother and with others. People I thought would remain close in my life moved out of relationship with me and surprisingly others who I hardly knew became close and intimate friends. The words I sensed of going back to Ohio and bringing disruption to my relationships proved true. Those disruptions started a series of events that disqualified my great fears and validated my courage in returning to Ohio.

By the spring of 2005, I had become a worship leader at a local church and was preparing to act as interim music director while the church interviewed men to replace the previous music director. I was also in transition in relocating into the city. I needed a place to live temporarily until my apartment was ready and asked my mother if I could stay with her for a short time. Her excitement was surprising. She quickly invited me to stay and even suggested that I save money by staying with her on a long-term basis. At the time, I realized had grown a great deal but I figured I had much more work to do before I could consider that idea.

Within a week of moving in with my mother, our surface conversations and topics gained more depth and honesty. I began asking her questions about her youth and childhood. My mother remained cautious in her responses but seemed to take more risks in being vulnerable. I also began to take small steps in talking about my care for people and my passions in seeing people move toward their dreams and potential. The more I let down my guard, the more I started discovering weaknesses and vulnerabilities in my mother that I loved seeing.

Instead of fear, I was beginning to enjoy the company of this woman I feared and resented for so long. Years before, I had forgiven her of past abuse and the harmful words she had said to me. I needed no apology or confession of wrongdoing for me to move in cautious relationship with her. My boundary with her was the refusal of harm that I no longer would accept. To witness not only a change in her personality but an effort to heal our relationship, came as a total surprise to me. Our conversations and the new direction of honesty were the first indication that maybe there was a plan in bringing me back and it had to do with mom and me.

I remember the first time she told me she loved me. I was in the process of getting ready for bed. As I walked up the stairs to my room, my mother cautiously said, "Have a good night. I love you." I nearly fell up the stairs. I could not believe my ears. Her words were foreign to me. A silence cut through the air. I did not know how to respond but I replied, "Good night, love you too." I was very uncomfortable in saying those words to her. I could say tender words of affection and love to others. However, speaking those words to my mother felt strange.

During a warm weekend in December of 2005, I returned home from church and found my mother in bed complaining of horrible stomach pains. She had a high tolerance to pain, so once it became unbearable for her I knew I needed to take her to the emergency room. At the hospital, doctors discovered she had pancreatitis and a small mass growing inside of her. They kept her overnight to run further tests regarding the mass they found. I received a call the next day from the doctors telling me the mass in my mother was third stage pancreatic cancer.

My mother died on the afternoon of Sunday, August 6, 2006. My sister and aunt were with me by her side and witnessed her last breath. I spoke words to her in the moments before she died and during our journey together that I will never reveal to anyone. Only God knows the purposes and plans of moving me back to Ohio.

When I moved back, I could not see anything outside of my perspective and fears. I will never fully know, on this side of Heaven, all the purposes and plans when I was called to leave the comfort of my life in Nashville. However, I know if I had allowed my fears to prevent me from returning to Ohio, I would not have experienced the renewed relationship and friendship with my mother or been forever changed by the growth that took place.

STEPPING ON THE BACK OF FEAR

Fear is not the real problem or the enemy: Fear is no more of a problem standing in the way than a person who harmed someone in the past is a true obstacle from moving forward. The fear feels strong, just as the memories and pain of the past feel strong. However, we have the power to choose reality over feelings and truth over lies. We also have the power and choice to make fear a problem or use it to prompt us forward in courage.

Fear is not the real problem. Believing that in order to dream we have to be fearless is the real problem. Fear is a simple emotion that is an indicator of something. The only power fear has, like any other emotion, is the power that we give it to make choices in our lives.

The goal in moving forward is not about getting rid of fear: Imagine the owner of a company deciding that he needed to change his eating habits. Each day he entered the building's doors to see employees eating in the company dining area. When he rode the elevators to his office, he noticed people chewing gum, drinking soft drinks and enjoying things that were not on his diet plan. When the company owner passed the break room to enter his office he saw the vending machine filled with snacks and treats.

One day, the owner decided that the only way for him to move forward was to rid himself of his perceived problem. He went into the office the next day and had all food, drinks, and vending machines removed from the building.

That action does not make too much sense. However, we often believe similar thoughts regarding fear. If we could just get rid of the problem, then everything would be all right. If we could only get rid of fear from our lives or stop fearing then we would easily grab hold of our dreams and goals.

Remember, fear is just a simple feeling of indication. It has no power and cannot make any choices. Fear is not the problem so there is no need to be rid of its deeds. Resisting fear only strengthens it.

Instead of giving time to a mere feeling and offer it power, try simply walking in courage that is moving forward in spite of fear. No one who has ever achieved great things or accomplished big dreams was noted as being fearless. The greatness of their character was that in spite of fear, obstacles, their pasts, and other dream stealers, they continued to walk in courage fighting to reach their dream.

Eight Practical Tips

The Prevention magazine article, "What are you afraid of? Eight secrets that make fear disappear"3 offer these tips for dealing with everyday fears:

1. It doesn't matter why you're scared. Knowing why you've developed a particular fear doesn't do much to help you overcome it, and it delays your progress in areas that will actually help you become less afraid. Stop trying to figure it out.

2. Learn about the thing you fear. Uncertainty is a huge component of fear: Developing an understanding of what you're afraid of goes a long way toward erasing that fear.

3. Train. If there's something you're afraid to try because it seems scary or difficult, start small, and work in steps. Slowly building familiarity with a scary subject makes it more manageable.

4. Find someone who is not afraid. If there's something you're afraid of, find someone who is not afraid of that thing and spend time with that person. Take her along when you try to conquer your fear -- it'll be much easier.

5. Talk about it. Sharing your fear out loud can make it seem much less daunting.

6. Play mind games. If you're afraid of speaking in front of groups, it's probably because you think the audience is going to judge you. Try imagining the audience members naked -- being the only clothed person in the room puts you in the position of judgment.

7. Stop looking at the grand scheme. Think only about each successive step. If you're afraid of heights, don't think about being on the fortieth floor of a building. Just think about getting your foot in the lobby.

8. Seek help. Fear is not a simple emotion. If you're having trouble overcoming your fear on your own, find a professional to help you.

CHAPTER SIX

DREAM STEALER #2-THE PAST
"The past is a foreign country; they do things differently there."

---- L. P. Hartley (1895–1972)

Because it takes a professional to help with deep-seated issues, long-term effects, and healing, we will not deal in depth with messages and memories from the past. However, we do want to understand the relationship between possible past messages and how they might be stealing our dreams and hopes for the future.

According to information regarding areas of the past from the 2010 survey, fifty percent of people surveyed believed they "would be okay if the abuse, trauma, hurt, etc. never happened" in their lives. Fifty-two percent of people believed "life should be fair."

Why are we so hard and believe so little in ourselves? Why do we believe our mistakes, hurts, and negative situations of the past are scars to be covered and hidden? What has taken place to turn the little girl or boy who once Dreamed Madly, Pursued Wildly and Trusted Completely into the adult man or woman who now uncomfortably settles for lost dreams, remains in safety and trusts no one? What has happened to that little girl and boy? What has happened to those dreams and bright eyes? What happened in your past?

A huge dream stealer is the past. Daily, I counsel, speak before, and talk with people who truly believe their negative pasts predicate a negative future. Often people will play out the pain in their lives and unresolved issues from their pasts through addictions, acting out, obsessions, fantasy, avoidance, religious behavior, and hopelessness. It is so easy to believe there is no purpose, no future, or hope when all a person has known are failure, obstacles, and negative comments.

Some continue to work through many unresolved issues but find it difficult to move forward due to filters of past or present situations. We say things like, "I just lost my job," "I have a family," "I'm too old," "I don't have a degree in …," "I am in bad health," "I'm a single mother," "I failed at things before," "I was a drug addict," or "I was in jail." Each of those perceived limitations is a lie we have bought into to steal our dreams.

THE LIE BOUGHT INTO

From the person living on the streets or in prison to the supermodel, celebrity, or candidate for the White House, each one of us has a past. Some of us have a past filled with stories of pain, sadness, and losses while others have pasts filled with stories of wonderful relationships, happy memories, and joys. Regardless of the events, dreams are stolen due to the beliefs and messages we created based on the past.

No matter how we grew up, as humans, we desire to hide the mistakes, failures, hurts, habits and the hang-ups in our lives. We are all human and walk among the wounded.

The problem is not that we were wounded or even that we failed or were harmed. The problem is that we bought into the huge lie that there was a problem with being wounded or failing. They were lies we picked up somewhere between the insecurity of a father's rage, the immaturity of a school mate's shout, or the good intentions of an overly protective relative. We bought into the lie that because we were placed in a position of responsibility, we always have to be the responsible one or because we failed at something we were a failure.

What is the conclusion most people make when they hear that someone or something is wounded or broken? More often than not, some would conclude the person or thing is in bad shape, perhaps has an addiction, was abused, is living on the streets, has a negative past, is unwanted, has a lower value, etc.

So often we jump to the conclusion that being wounded is equal to being unusable, unfixable, permanent, and shameful, something we should hide or not talk about, a weakness, a flaw or something unnatural. The fact is we are all wounded to various degrees simply because we are fallible humans capable of hurting others and being hurt.

By definition, the word "wound" simply means, *"an injury to the body or a mental or emotional hurt or blow."*[1] In other words, if we have ever been hurt, misunderstood, betrayed, harmed, lost someone or suffered loss, been rejected, disappointed, etc. we have experienced wounds in our lives. Often but not always, because of that wound the view in which we see ourselves and others gets blurred through the filter of our experience.

For example, if at some point in a person's life they were told, "You're not going to be successful in life," they will subconsciously create a view of themselves and others. Depending on many factors, that person may grow up believing what they were told and fail to live up to their potential or they may become very successful simply to prove the person wrong.

Being wounded simply means we are not perfect and because of being human and living life, situations and experiences have happened that affect the way we view our world. That impact created a believed or real obstacle that stands between where we are and where we want to be (our dreams and visions).

Realizing we have wounds and dream-stealers from the past does not mean we are weak, less than, problematic or an outcast. Instead, we can realize we are not perfect, while being real with others, and allow our experiences to push us toward our potential instead of holding us in captive. It is difficult but it is possible.

I remember hearing a story about a woman from Nebraska who was raised from age six, for the most part, in a small trailer by a lake. Outcast from her peers and poor, she often said the only time she felt accepted was when she was reading a book or play acting. When she was 13, her parents divorced. Despite her desperate poverty, being an outcast and child of divorce, she had a dream. She had a dream that would call for great sacrifice, loss and points of living out of a car. Still, despite being labeled what other might call homeless, poor, not good enough, etc. she refused to allow her past to be a dream stealer. She was an example of someone who knew the task was difficult but also believed the dream was possible.

MESSAGES OF THE PAST

Somewhere in our lives we began to exchange what we felt for who we were, and in that moment our dreams became too hard to capture. Our hopes slowly turned into things we could easily obtain. Our trust was relegated to a world we believed we could control. Maybe the feelings of being so overwhelmed with shame and guilt from the past allowed us to believe there was nothing we could add to the world or maybe the world would be better without us. Yeah, I get that.

We can easily tell of the present scars and issues resulting from the past but often we don't connect our behaviors and choices to past hurts and messages we've received. Like fear, the dream stealer of the past did not suddenly appear. This dream stealer has had years of practice and experience in holding back potential in our lives.

So what can we do to take the power away from the past and uncover some of the mysteries that linger in our current lives? We can start by getting a better understanding of why some issues from the past still haunt us. Further, we can make some connections to messages we received from the past that we still believe today.

Before we begin an exercise that will help to uncover some connections, let me say again, nothing written in this book or its exercises should replace the advice and counsel of a personal and professional psychologist or psychiatrist specialized for your specific needs. I not only encourage seeking the counsel of a licensed therapist but also I endorse that relationship with someone whom you can meet and work with in person.

A few methods are helpful in dealing with messages that have led to current beliefs. The method I have found most helpful in identifying my past messages and in working with clients has been through diagramming the messages we received.

Messages are signals or meanings we ascribe to people and experiences in our lives. For example, let's say you were invited to coffee by an acquaintance from work. During your time together, the acquaintance occasionally glances at his cell phone to check the time. You might receive a message from his behavior that he is not interested in spending time with you or he would rather be somewhere else.

You receive and assume different messages until the other person finally shares he has a medical condition that requires medication at prescribed times. You received a message based on certain assumptions. An interpretation of the situation created messages you held onto until further information offered a new perspective.

The same situation happens in each of our lives. Daily we receive messages, good and bad, that are based on signals and meaning we ascribe to our experiences. A man catches a pretty woman looking at him twice in a store's checkout line. A message that man might receive is, "Hey, I'm the man and I'm attractive." A woman is passed over for a promotion and a younger woman is chosen. A message she might receive is, "I'm too old to be successful or worth a promotion."

As children and young adults, our minds are not able to analyze the messages or separate fact from fiction. A possible message a child could receive after being cussed at by a parent might be, "I am worthless and don't deserve to be valued." The child is not able to reason that the problem is with the angry parent or that the parent is acting out of anger and frustration. The child simply receives a message that he or she cannot interpret and internalizes it. The message becomes a belief about him or her and the world. Until the message offers clarification, it continues to grow and become more a part of the beliefs of the child and attaches to his or her identity.

Messages, similar to assumptions, are not facts. They are only our interpretation and a judgment call. However, messages differ from assumptions in that the judgment call is about us as a person. Assumptions often but not always make a judgment call about someone, something else as well as us...

If someone significant in our lives passes without saying something we could easily assume they were upset or putting on airs. A message someone could receive from the same situation is "Something is wrong with me or I did something to offend them."

Our messages usually make us the focus, whereas assumptions make another person, situation, or object, as well as ourselves, the focus.

MESSAGES EXERCISE

Now that we have a better understanding of what messages are, let's see what messages we might have received from the past that deter our dreams for the future.

On Page 187, you will find a diagram called "Messages of the Past" with four sections. For now, we will be working with the top portion of the diagram called "The Past."

On the top of the page, there are six boxes in a row. This section is for listing the people, situations, and things said in our past that influenced us in positive and negative ways. A sample is available on Page 188 to assist with the exercise.

The first two boxes are for people (people columns), the second two are for situations (situation columns), and the last two are for words that were said (words said columns), that influenced us either positive or negative way. An example of a person could be a parent, friend, abuser, relative, stranger, great teacher, neighbor, etc. Examples of situations are "bullied at school," "wonderful birthday party," "having alcoholic parents," "life at home," or "having wealth." Examples of words said are being told you were a loser, being told you could do anything, "You're my favorite daughter," "You're lazy," etc.

Although difficult, try to remain objective in writing down the facts instead of the personal feelings attached. We will add the feelings, emotions, and beliefs in the next section. For now, simply write, "Father," "Teacher," "Bullied at school," "Spoiled as child," "Told I was a loser," "Came from money" instead of "A father who was a pig," "An amazing teacher," "Everybody called me a loser," "I could buy whatever I wanted," etc.

Here are some tips in filling out the boxes of this section:

1. There only two boxes for each type so think of major influencers. I have known a particular family member all my life who was also one of my abusers but he did not influence me greatly outside of the abuse. Think of a person, situation, or thing that has a deep emotion (good or bad) tied to it. Something you believe was a life-changing type of impact.

2. If you begin to become anxious, depressed or experience great difficulty while doing this exercise, stop. The point of this exercise and chapter is to connect some dream stealers regarding the past to obstacles for future dreams. The intent is not to replace therapy or open up wounds that cannot be managed through this book. If you are in that situation, please seek someone safe to talk to, preferably a professional. There is no shame in that. It's difficult to move forward if you still

are fighting with the past. Please get help first, and then come back to this.

3. Try not to judge your past. Ironically, some feel their pasts are less important because they have less drama or tragedy. Anyone who has been blessed enough to have had limited drama and negative situations should be incredibly grateful for that fact. Please don't let society's influence leave you believing anything less than the story you have lived is wrong. In a later chapter, we will discuss our stories and their influence on our dreams. For now, try not to judge your past and hold onto the fact that whatever your story is, it is important.

After completing the top section of six boxes, it is time to move to the next section called "Received Messages." In this section, we will begin to make some connections between the people, situations, and words said in the past to messages we interpreted from them.

Under the people columns, begin to write down messages or signals you received about yourself from those people, whether positive or negative. An example of some possible messages from a loving mother might be, "I am lovable," "I am acceptable," "I am enjoyable," etc. An example of some possible messages from an abuser might be, "I am worthless," "I'm not lovable," "I am only to be used by others," etc.

Write down as many messages as you can think of on the lines under the people column. When you are finished, go to the situation columns, do the same, and follow with the words said columns. If you begin to feel overwhelmed during the exercise, please stop. For some, it is helpful to have a safe person to do the exercise with in order to get some feedback and objectivity.

We will continue to fill out the remainder of the exercise as we continue to expose the stealers of our dreams. In the next chapter, we will move forward into the third section to connect the messages we received with the feelings and beliefs we created.

THE TRUTH ABOUT THE PAST

1. **Your past has a purpose**. Our past is simply a combination of themes, passions, burdens, and events that offer hints to the purpose and dreams of the future. Our past does not define us but does affect our choices and influences our direction and path. The best is yet to come.

2. **The past can't hurt you anymore unless you allow it.** Remember, if you have been through a difficult or harmful past, you have endured the worst part and survived. Despite your feelings and fears, you are more courageous than you might realize. The past is simply that, the past and not the present. I am not referring to the grief and healing process that will continue to take place. The people, places and things that

caused the original hurt can no longer hurt you like before. Of course, if you are still in the same environment with a past offender or situation that has caused harm, my suggestion would be to seek the authorities or wise counsel.

3. **Your past is not the enemy**.

Our past, like pain, is not the enemy. It is nothing to be feared, hidden or disguised. Learn from it. The past has no power at all unless we allow it to be used to steal and kill the dreams that have been placed in us.

The woman from Nebraska who refused to allow the dream stealer of her past, poverty, rejection, and home life to deter her from her dream was Hillary Swank. In 1999, she won her first Oscar for *Boys Don't Cry*, and then captured a second one in 2004 for *Million Dollar Baby*. After winning her second Oscar, she said, "I don't know what I did in this life to deserve this. I'm just a girl from a trailer park who had a dream."[2]

CHAPTER SEVEN

DREAM STEALER #3-EMOTIONS
"The degree of one's emotions varies inversely with one's knowledge of the facts."

---- **Bertrand Russell (1872–1970)**

I absolutely love the movie *The Matrix*. The sequels were fine, but to me, neither of them compared to the original. In the original *Matrix*, Morpheus (played by Laurence Fishburne) asks Neo (played by Keanu Reeves) to choose either the red pill or the blue pill. When Neo asks what the Matrix is, Morpheus tells him (**you have to read this in a very deep and impending-doom voice**):

"The Matrix is a prison for your mind. Unfortunately, no one can be told what the Matrix is. You have to see it for yourself. After this, there is no turning back. You take the blue pill, the story ends; you wake up in your bed and believe whatever you want to believe. You take the red pill, you stay in Wonderland, and I show you how deep the rabbit hole goes."[1]

Man, I love that! Although the movie is a work of fiction, it parallels our humanity throughout. In the movie, the Matrix was the computerized world that was false but people thought to be true. I compare the Matrix to our false world of feelings and filters (what we feel, often believe, etc.) versus the truth of who we really are and what our lives are meant to be.

An example of this is someone who has lived a past of abuse or trauma. Often they will view themselves and the world around them through the skewed image of their false world and believe they are destined to fail or not accomplish great things. That's their current false world they believe to be true. That is a dream stealer of emotions shutting down their dreams and hopes.

However, what would happen if they started to grab hold, or make the decision to take that "red pill," start reading their story, walking in courage based on who they truly were, and began to dream and hope again for their future and accomplished great things? The results would be life changing.

Emotions, including fear, can act as dream stealers in our path if we allow them to. If everything (outside of uncontrollable things such as breathing, when we die, significant emotional events, etc.) is a choice, then we have the power to choose to give in to this dream stealer or not.

Like fear, the goal in dealing with the dream stealer of emotions is not to rid ourselves of the so-called problem but to understand what it is and how it impacts our lives.

FEELINGS, NOTHING MORE THAN FEELINGS

Does this scenario sound familiar? You're driving down the highway and someone cuts you off, barely missing your car. You veer to the side out of fear of getting hit and find that your heart feels as though it is beating outside of your chest. How dare they do that! You get angry and drive faster in order to pull up next to the person to give them a piece of your mind, or at least throw them the evil eye of disapproval.

When you see the driver, you realize that not only is he or she unfazed by what happened but he or she also fails to have a bit of remorse for disrupting your safe and peaceful drive. However, you did something. You were hurt (which often we won't admit) and angry and you did something to let the other person know you were not happy about it.

Yeah, I've been there myself. I have even dreamed of having the ability to have the highway patrol at my disposal to immediately track down and arrest anyone I felt was an affront to the rules of the road. My would-be road violations would not count, of course.

The point is situations and life happen every day that cause us to feel angry, tired, worn out, burned out and sometimes even wanting out. Between the unemployment rate, government issues, the BP gulf crisis, job loss, and just plain old life, it's easy to simply say, "Okay, enough of this. I have had it!"

So often we are busy reacting and doing things that we miss the great lesson of growth in just being. We get so busy putting our energy into getting back at the co-worker who sold us out for a promotion or planning ways to be a more impressive person so that the leader, organization, whoever will choose us over someone else next time. That's a whole lot of energy being used for a small reason.

I have found that in the midst of feeling our emotions we miss understanding what our emotions (which are simply indicators of something and nothing more) are trying to tell us.

Before we can move forward to what we want to do, we really need to gain a better understand of why we do what we do and our motivation for it. Our emotions are NOT our enemy; they are simply indicators that something is going on.

When I was sixteen years old a song based on a melody composed by Loulou Gaste and sung by Morris Albert was popular on the radio. The name of the song was *Feelings*. Although years have come and gone, the opening line of the song remains with me. The first words were, "Feelings, nothing more than feelings." Never has a song told more truth through fewer words.

Our feelings are truly nothing more than feelings, indicators that something else is going on with our world and us. We often give our feelings, which are not synonymous with emotions, power they do not have. Our feelings are important. However, the larger umbrella that covers our feelings is our emotions.

A feeling is an emotional reaction or state, while emotions, according to Merriam-Webster Dictionary, are a *"conscious mental reaction (as anger or fear) subjectively experienced as strong feeling usually directed toward a specific object and* *typically accompanied by physiological and behavioral changes in the body."*2

Feelings are often temporary and calm down or disappear once the issue is no longer present, whereas emotions will stay with us for years because they are seated in our mind. Further, feelings are triggered by external stimuli like physical sensations as well as mental states, but emotions come from our mind. So if emotions come from inside a person rather than from observation or outside stimulus, a body would respond to the emotions with ... feelings.

Our feelings can come from reacting with any of our five senses. The result is feelings of warmth, hunger, thirst, chill, dryness, sadness, happiness, excitement, fear, disgust, or hurt.

Emotions are generally categorized by degree. Because of this, you could say that the biggest difference between feelings and emotions is that feelings have to be triggered by an external motivating factor whereas emotions can be completely internalized.

For example, let's say our father is yelling at us. According to our beliefs (I'll never do anything right, I am never wrong, or another belief), we translate that situation with our feelings. The feeling we experience from the interpretation is an emotion (anger, fear, sadness, etc).

Several emotional theories state that there are six primary emotions that are common to all cultures: love, anger, happiness, sorrow, anticipation, and fear. Note: Anger often takes a lead among the emotion dream stealers. When we experience a perceived loss of control over things that are important to us in some way, we feel angry. That loss of control could look like unemployment, failure, past issues, or a comparison to another person who is achieving things or goals we desire. We assume others have the control we feel we are lacking and become angry.

Our emotions are not positive or negative. They are a response that propels us either forward or backward.

A complication in human emotion is the fact that we have memories. Our memories, along with the memories of others, can carry an emotional load for us and cause us to feel several conflicting emotions simultaneously. Charles B. Parselle states, "The worst thing that can be said about an emotion is that it may be inappropriate to the present situation because past emotions may be carried forward in time."[3]

Our emotions are indicators that are a normal part of our lives. Unfortunately, we have been told that emotions, like sadness, are bad and we needed to deny them together with our feelings. Our emotions are indicators that need a proper release. When we suppress (hold in) our emotions, it often leads to depression. When we repress (lock away) our emotions, it often leads to illness. When we deny (don't deal with) our emotions, it often leads to issues of integrity.

Over time, our emotions create a state of habit, something we begin to trust in as truth. We might receive a message from a parent who always catered to our needs and gave us what we wanted that "I can have anything I want." The feelings we could have from that message might be pride, superiority, favored status, etc. Over time, those feelings and emotions become beliefs about the world and us.

MESSAGES EXERCISE

Now that we have a better understanding of emotions and beliefs, let's see how they have possibly deterred our dreams for the future.

Return to the "Messages of the Past" diagram on Page 187. We will be working with the third portion of the diagram, called "Feelings and Beliefs." In this section, we will begin to make some connections between the messages we interpreted from people of influence in our past to feelings, emotions, and beliefs we have that might be dream stealers.

Under the area where you have listed two people, begin to write down feelings, emotions, and beliefs you had (or have) about those messages you received from them. Example: If I have received messages that I am only acceptable when I am achieving or performing well, I might feel worthless when I am not achieving or working or I might not feel acceptable when I make a mistake or don't reach expectations. That is a normal response.

Sometimes feelings get confused with thoughts. To assist you with this exercise, a list of feeling words is available beginning on Page 189 as a guide to help identify actual feelings versus thoughts as you continue.

Write down as many feelings, emotions, and beliefs as you can think of on the lines under the people column. When you are finished, go to the situation column, do the same, and follow with the "words said" column. As a reminder, if you begin to feel overwhelmed during the exercise, please stop. It is often helpful to have a safe person do the exercise with you in order to offer some feedback and objectivity.

We will continue to fill out the remainder of the exercise as we continue to expose the stealers of our dreams. In Chapter Eight, we will move to the final section to connect the feelings, emotions, and beliefs with the actions and dream stealers we have allowed in our lives.

EMOTIONS – THE DREAM STEALER

Emotions are not dream stealers because they are a problem in and of themselves. Again, emotions are neither good nor bad, although they may have a negative or positive feeling attached to them. Emotions become dream stealers when we attach them to our identity and make what we feel who we are.

Emotions become dream stealers when we allow the emotions (shame, guilt, worthlessness, superiority, etc.) of our life to dictate our decisions, attitudes, movements, and hopes in dreaming for more and living out our potential. We often give power to emotions in making them controllers of our lives instead of seeing them as indicators of situations or internal problems that should be dealt with accordingly.

The dream stealer of emotions has many different faces and reveals itself in our lives in numerous ways. The following are a few ways emotional dream stealers reveal themselves:

- **Shame** – feeling bad about who we are because of something
- **Illegitimate Guilt** – feeling bad about something we did and not letting go of it after we have made amends
- **Rejection** – feeling others won't accept us because of something.
- **Comparison** – feeling we have less value than others
- **Unforgiveness** – feeling someone or something has to be accountable in order for us to move forward
- **Hurt self-image** – feeling our story or life is not effective, doesn't matter or doesn't have value
- **Negative skewed filter** – feeling we are failures and have no story of worth
- **Positive skewed Filter** – feeling we wrote our own story and owe nothing

Here are some of the survey results regarding areas of our emotions.
Statement: **"I get jealous of others' happiness and success."**
Believed: Fifty-five percent

Statement: **"It's easy for me to find fault with myself and/or others."**
Believed: Seventy-four percent

Statement: **"I usually feel less than or that something's wrong with me."**
Believed: Fifty-eight percent

Statement: **"It is far more preferable to be strong than to be weak or vulnerable."**
Believed: Ninety-four percent

Statement: **"I get hurt easily"**
Believed: Sixty-one percent

Statement: **"It's better to hold in my emotions and anger than to let it all out."**
Believed: Fifty-seven percent

Statement: **"I often react based on how I feel."**
Believed: Sixty-eight percent

Statement: **"I have a tendency to take things personally."**
Believed: Seventy-one percent

Statement: **"I have a tendency to think in extremes (Either right or wrong, good or bad)."**
Believed: Fifty-three percent

Statement: **"When I am hurt or disappointed I feel I need to do something, eat or take something to feel better."**
Believed: Fifty-two percent

While an issue was clear in the percentage of people who believed the statements, the problem is that each of the statements given within the survey was based on lies, false beliefs, and emotional dream stealers. All of the statements lead to us choosing and allowing our emotions to immobilize us instead of taking our emotions captive and pushing forward. Time, healing, and help are the keys in taking those emotions captive without attempting to turn them off.

THE TRUTH ABOUT EMOTIONS

1. **Our feelings and emotions have no power outside of what we give them**. Regardless of the pain, harm, injustice, or confusion of our emotions, ultimately everything is a choice. In most cases, we were not able to have a choice in the situations done to us. However, as an adult, we do have the choice in how we deal with the impact of those situations.

2. **Our feelings and emotions are not problems but symptoms of a possible problem in our lives**.

3. **Our feelings and emotions are only feelings and emotions, they are never who we are as a person.**

4. **Our feelings and emotions are not the enemy**.

Although emotional dream stealers can get in the way of our journey in Dreaming Madly, Pursuing Wildly, and Trusting Completely, another dream stealer often shuts us down before we begin. That dream stealer comes in the form of people.

CHAPTER EIGHT

DREAM STEALER #4-PEOPLE
"I judge people by what they might be,—not are, nor will be."

---- **Robert Browning, English poet.** *A Soul's Tragedy,* Act II

Recently, a casual acquaintance asked me out for coffee. I had return to Nashville, Tennessee, after spending four months in Dallas, Texas. We were not close but she was familiar with bits and pieces of my life and had a vague idea of my dreams, or at least I thought she did. When she called me unexpectedly, my suspicion was that she was more curious than caring about why I returned to Nashville and my plans for the near future. She assumed, like a few others, that my travel back to Nashville was due to a position or explainable reason that would justify my return.

We met for coffee (tea, in my case) and began with the usual light topic conversations about changes in the city, updates at the church and general events and changes in our lives during my absence. After twenty minutes of familiarities, she asked the question: "So, Charlotte, why are you back in Nashville?" I first explained the set of circumstances that led to my sudden return to Nashville.

I told her of the incredible discovery that took place during my time in Dallas and how my life changed from when I originally left Nashville. I mentioned the unexpected doors that closed and the many open doors and clarity of direction I had in moving toward the vision and dream before me. Finally, I told her about the events of Thursday morning that confirmed to me that it was time to return to Nashville.

The acquaintance seemed interested but not satisfied by my story of making such a sudden and dramatic move back. She looked at me, crossed her arms, and said, "Hmm!"

Unfortunately, my curiosity and pride got the better of me and I asked, "So what is going through your head?" That is a question I often reserve for others to ponder thoughts and feelings about themselves. Foolishly, I asked the question that I would later regret asking. She was eager to respond.

She looked down and said, "Charlotte, you seem clueless." Of course, my automatic reaction was to jump across the table and grab her by the neck but it was a public place and I feared being the lead story in the newspaper the next morning. She continued with her thoughts and feelings of why my reasoning was off and why it was time to stop dreaming for something more and settle down for something "concrete."

Although I was hurt and regretted opening up to someone who was not a safe person, I considered the source, her personal issues regarding the risk of dreaming, and told her, "Thank you for the coffee. You don't know me well enough to place judgment on my life, and let's just agree that we don't agree." I said a polite goodbye while we talked about the construction changes on the street and walked to our cars.

Dream stealer #4 is people.

Dream Stealer #4 - People

Humans have the ability to procreate and have a brain that science in all its research and knowledge have still not been able to fully understand or duplicate perfectly or naturally. Unlike any other creature, humans have a unique set of qualities that set us apart.

We have the quality of sympathy. We offer sympathy for others by sharing one's feeling of sorrow or pain. When we are sympathetic towards a person, we feel pity or feel sorry for them but do not necessarily understand what they are actually feeling.

Another unique quality that humans have is empathy. Showing empathy toward a person requires one to be open-minded and compassionate enough to experience the pain of what somebody else is going through. With empathy, to an extent, we are putting ourselves in the person's place, have a good sense of how they feel, and understand their feelings to some degree.

We have the quality of morality. To have the quality of morality makes us capable of distinguishing between what is good and evil. Morality is practicing the right ethics in your personal and professional life even while no one is watching.

Forgiveness is another unique quality we have as humans. Forgiveness offers a message of "Debt paid" toward others for their acts that have harmed or hurt us. When we forgive, we give the other person undeserved grace. More importantly, forgiveness allows us to move from being a victim to being a survivor and from being a powerless person to one who is empowered.

Although we have unique qualities to offer help, support, encouragement, understanding, and forgiveness, people often intentionally and unintentionally offer another unique quality that has become a great dream stealer. We cut off the dreams of others through our own pain and struggles. In short, we have the ability to hurt people.

HURT PEOPLE HURT PEOPLE

A frustrated blue-collar father kicked around by his boss comes home to his seven-year-old boy. After years of trying to get ahead and falling short, the father arrives at the conclusion that only the rich and well connected can get ahead in life. In a moment of imagination, the young boy runs to his father exclaiming his excitement in desiring to be a big news reporter when he grows up just like the man he saw on television. The father shouts, "Stop dreaming, boy! You're going to grow up to be nothing, just like me."

One by one, dreams are stolen through people who project their own pain and frustrations onto the ears and lives of others. People who are dream stealers live as land dwellers, only seeing what is in front of them. Often they will wait until a dreamer or visionary paves the way so they call walk a road that someone has prepared.

People who are dream stealers are easy to identify. Usually they are the ones blaming everyone and Santa Claus as to why their life is not working and they are not able to have a wonderful future of possibilities. They are often dissatisfied with their own lives and find it easier to be a stumbling block for someone instead of finding ways to improve their own.

People who are dream stealers watch others succeed while they live vicariously through the dreamer's life or complain about how they would have accomplished or done things differently. It is much easier to sit on the sidelines watching an Oprah Winfrey or a Bill Gates and making opinions about their actions than it is to become an Oprah Winfrey or Bill Gates in their own right in whatever shape that takes.

They see through the limited eyes of the obtainable and only trust in what they believe they can control. If a risk is required, they choose safety. If trust is required, they choose control. If imagination is required, they choose what is common and known. If hope is required, they choose to settle. Their world is often limited because their hope is also limited.

People who are dream stealers are not bad people or even mean people. They are simply limited in their view of what is possible and in turn impose that limitation on others. Often they are not dream stealers because they intend to be but because they are hurt in some way. Their hurt in turn hurts others. This does not justify their actions but offers understanding.

These dream stealers can be vicious and intentional in causing hurt or they can be completely oblivious to the words or actions they use. They can shout words predicting the impotent future of someone or give gentle words of opinion believing it is in the best interest of another.

I will never forget the calm words of a pastor who told me I was damaged goods and God would never use me because of my past of abuse and other issues. I truly believe that in his mind he offered those words as his version of help in telling me to be realistic due to my limitations. Unknowingly, that pastor's words were dream stealers.

For years, I believed that he knew best because of his position of authority and knowledge. I believed and accepted his words as true because of the negative filters I saw the world through and the distorted mirror that reflected an image that accepted I was damaged goods and unusable due to my past.

That pastor unknowingly acted as a dream stealer in my life until I stole my dreams back. Instead of being a curse and a dream stealer, his words, in part, have helped me to author two books regarding damaged goods, speak to audiences nationally, and create a passion to help people Dream Madly.

Regardless of the people who act as dream stealers in our lives, the choice always remains with us as to whether we will allow them to stop or hinder our dreams. All too often, we allow them consciously and subconsciously to thwart dreams, desires, goals and movement toward a life that matters.

THE AUTOMATIC REACTION

Dream Stealer #4 - People

Daily the impact of people's words and actions steals dreams and in turn gives us a type of automatic reaction to the world around us. Some of those reactions were clear on the 2010 survey regarding areas were people viewed others with a power they never had.

Sixty-one percent of people responded yes to the statement, "I am afraid to confront people who I think will reject me." Fifty-two percent were afraid of abandonment from people. Another fifty-two percent answered yes to "People can't handle the real me." A whopping one hundred percent believed that "People can make me mad or happy at times."

The last statement may have surprised you as being a lie or false statement. We will deal with the survey and its results in Chapter 11. For now understand the link to all of the dream stealers we are dealing with in this book. The link is that none of them has any power outside of what we give them despite the strong feelings, emotions, and beliefs we have attached to them.

Just as the statement "I had no choice" is inaccurate, the statement, "He (she) made me sad or angry" is equally inaccurate. There is no force to feel anything we are not choosing first to feel unless by intimidation. For example, here is a situation near and dear to most of our hearts: You are driving on the highway with a car full of passengers during rush hour. You use your turn signal to make a move to the left lane. Just as you are about to move, a speeding driver with no regard for others' safety dashes into your left lane, almost sideswiping you, and passes without an apology.

First, take a breath. Second, the immediate feeling is anger and a realization that the driver did not care about your life or the lives of your passengers. After a few choice words and some yelling, one of the passengers asks, "Why are you so upset?" You respond, "Because that driver made me mad!"

The reason why the statement on the survey was false was that in that situation and in every situation, people do things that impact us negatively and positively. A feeling rises in us and we attach the source of that feeling to someone or something. Continually, we are left asking ourselves, "Am I sad, or is the other person or thing bad?" Was that driver evil and intentionally trying to cut me off and hurt me, or am I feeling hurt and angry because I felt like my life didn't matter to the driver and less valued?

In either case, neither the driver nor anyone else has the power to make us feel anything. People do and say things that impact us in ways that might cause hurt, happiness, sadness, etc. However, how we choose to feel and react to them and what they say is totally on us.

Contrary to the phrase, "The devil made me do it," made popular by comedian Flip Wilson's signature character Geraldine Jones, no, the devil doesn't make us do it. Furthermore, echoing the true words of Bonnie Raitt's song, "I can't make you love me if you don't"[1] the fact is we have no control to make anyone feel anything and they have no control over us.

The automatic reaction to people who are dream stealers and statements believed on the survey can easily create ways of self-protection that can shut down our dreams. In some cases, we become dream stealers in others' lives. In a great many cases, we internalize the words of dream stealers as truth and fail to move forward in capturing our dreams.

"AIN'T GOING TO LET NOBODY STEAL MY DREAM"

Of all of the dream stealers, people can stand out as one of the strongest and most oppressive. People have attempted to steal others' dreams since time began and will continue until time, as we know it is no more. We often recognize the angry words of a parent or guardian or the actions of an abuser or drunken driver as dream stealers. However, people's attempts to steal dreams come in many forms we may not realize.

Attempts to steal dreams come in the form of judgments of groups or certain types of people that set limitations regarding what potential is possible. Another attempt comes in the form of discrimination against groups or certain types of people that sets obstacles and disqualifications regarding what opportunities and dreams are possible. Many people have tried to steal and kill dreams through limitations and prejudice. Many more have determined in the face of abuse, cruel words, limitations, prejudices and more that no one or nothing will steal away their dreams.

As you read the following true story of Carl Brashear, be encouraged. Let his story encourage and remind you that no person's words, curse, actions, limitations, judgment, prejudice or any attempts to steal your dreams are impossible to overcome. You will find that the greater the obstacle, the greater the dream and the greater level of character that will result.

This is the amazing story of Carl Brashear and an example of the many stories of dreamers past and present who, in spite of dream stealers, said, "I ain't going to let nobody steal my dream."

Carl Maxie Brashear was born on January 19, 1931, in Larue County, Kentucky, where he and his seven siblings endured the stereotypical upbringing of a large, impoverished family in the South.

Brashear enlisted in the United States Navy on February 25, 1948, shortly after the Navy had desegregated. He began to develop an interest in diving after watching a U.S. Navy master diver save a man's life. African Americans in the Navy during that time were often relegated to steward duty. Essentially, they prepared and served meals.

Brashear persuaded his commanding officer to let him in the diving pool, although it took some time. Even then, his shipmates would leave threatening notes on his bunk with vile racial slurs and threaten his life if he so much as dipped a toe into the diving pool.

He had to learn the elements of diving: not coming to the surface too fast, developing the stamina to dive more than 300 feet deep while wearing 300 pounds of equipment, condition his body to such elements as joint pains and "the bends," and, of course, the threats of his shipmates. Brashear would claw his way through the naval ranks with unbridled determination of one day becoming a U.S. Navy master diver, a position no other African American had achieved.

Despite it all, Brashear had a surplus of inspiration. He once said, "My father was my inspiration. He said, 'You get in there, Carl, and you fight. You be the best!' I didn't go outside my family looking for my inspiration. I had all I need right there."

By 1951, he was a master-at-arms and serving temporary additional duty at salvage diving school. By 1965, aboard the USS Shakori, he became the ship's chief boatswain's mate, inching his way up the ranks. Soon he became leading diver, then underway officer of deck, followed by acting master diver and in-port duty chief.

Then, the unthinkable occurred. Brashear would encounter the most intensely painful and assuredly career-threatening experience of his life.

In 1966, the Air Force lost a nuclear bomb off the coast of Palomares, Spain. The Navy went to recover the bomb. After locating the bomb, Brashear and his underwater crew eventually brought it part way to the surface. The boat broke loose and the mooring line became disengaged, threatening the immediate safety of everyone in the area. Brashear began shoving sailors out of the way before a pipe came loose, flew across the deck, and smashed his leg below the knee, causing multiple fractures.

Out to sea with no doctor and no morphine, Brashear had to settle for two tourniquets. He was lifted to a different boat and scheduled to be shipped via helicopter to a nearby facility in Torrejon.

Brashear's foot became infected with gangrene before they transferred him to a German hospital where doctors told him it would be three years before they could have him walking with a brace. Brashear's desire and determination to complete his dream of becoming a master diver was so strong, he requested to be transferred to the United States, where doctors said they would cut his recovery time to 30 months. That was not good enough for Brashear, so he gave the okay to amputate.

And for Brashear, whose toughness astounded the doctors, it was not the loss of the lower part of his leg that bothered him. He was more concerned with when he could return to diving, a drive that doctors found almost humorous.

Brashear began reading books on amputees who had enjoyed postsurgical success and other books on how to maintain a healthy attitude despite his recent tragedy. After receiving a prosthetic leg, Brashear made good on his pledge to doctors that he would never use a crutch after that. Again they scoffed, and again he handed them a piece of wood and walked out of the hospital.

Getting no help from the physical education board and the naval hospitals, Brashear endorsed his own orders and reported to diving school. He was called back to the board and sent to spend a week at deep-sea diving school to see if he really was fit for duty. He performed before a captain, commander and various members of the medical board and was finally re-admitted to diving school.

Brashear was restored to master diver at the end of 1977. He retired from the Navy as a master diver and master chief petty officer on April 1, 1979. He attended college in Maryland and Virginia, studying environmental science. Brashear then worked for the government in various positions, including as an engineering technician and as an environmental protection specialist.

A film about Brashear, *Men of Honor*, finally hit the big screen in 2000. It starred Academy Award-winning actors Cuba Gooding Jr. and Robert DeNiro. It was directed by George Tillman Jr. and executive produced by Bill Cosby.

Carl Brashear will be remembered not only for being the first African American Navy diver, but as the man who faced tremendous odds and adversities, and won.

Brashear was motivated by his belief that "It's not a sin to get knocked down; it's a sin to stay down" and "I ain't going to let nobody steal my dream."[2]

CHAPTER NINE

DREAM STEALER #5-PERFORMANCE

"Once we realize that imperfect understanding is the human condition there is no shame in being wrong, only in failing to correct our mistakes."

---- George Soros (1730–)

As humans, we have needs. There are casual needs, which range from trivial to significant. They do not require relationship (e.g., "I need a new computer," "I need to eat three times per day instead of four," etc.). Casual needs are also wants or needs that do not greatly affect us if we do not receive them immediately.

There are critical needs, which are legitimate and important desires for quality relationships and additions to life (e.g., "I need to talk things over," "I need nurturing as a child," "I need relationships," etc.). Critical needs are important but often we deny them or put up walls to protect ourselves due to past relational hurts. While the need is vital, the fear of further pain can be greater, so we deny the need.

Finally, there are crucial needs that we did not create on our own. We are born with crucial needs and have them throughout our lives. Crucial needs are ingrained in us and they operate in our subconscious. Casual and critical needs are not. Our three crucial needs are the need to feel loved, the need to have worth, and the need to feel accepted. While casual and critical needs can be satisfied at a human level, crucial needs cannot.

Most interactions in our lives are an attempt to try to get one of those needs met or to avoid the pain of not getting a need met. For example, if I choose not to take on a big challenge or confront someone regarding an issue, often the reason is a fear of failure or rejection. A deeper reason is the fear that I will feel less worthy if I fail and feel less acceptable if someone rejects me.

Why is it important to know about our needs? Because as we begin to look at the dream stealer of performance we will need to gain an understanding of how our crucial needs influence our behavior and aid in creating performance-based identities that become dream stealers in our lives.

Before we talk about the dream stealer of performance, let's take a quick quiz. Respond yes or no to the following descriptive statements about yourself. Most of the statements have details to help explain them. Write down the total number of "yes" answers on a separate piece of paper. Be honest with your answers and try not to judge what is good or bad.

1. **There is a high need for control.**
    - Believe "Having control of __ will prevent me from being in pain."

2. **Frequently don't relate to your own feelings.**
    - You've learned to hide or ignore your feelings.
    - Expert at "stuffing them" because feeling hurts too much.

- Not showing feelings isn't the same as not having feelings.
- Basic statements: "I don't know what I feel"; "Whatever"; "I don't care."

3. **Seem to lose sense of yourself in people.**
   - Look for that lost love in all the wrong places and ways.
   - Attempt to meet legitimate needs in an illegitimate way.
   - Basic statements: "If he could only change, if he could love me right, then everything would be all right"; "If (name a person) were to die or leave me, I couldn't go on living."

4. **Highly aware of performance.**
   - Have to work for three crucial needs (worth, acceptance and love) to be met
   - Basic statements: "I'm acceptable when…"; "When I get this job I'll be happy"; "I'll be okay once I make a certain amount of money."

5. **Get possessive in relationships.**
   - Difficult to find line where you end and other person begins.
   - Consume others to fulfill own needs.
   - Afraid of losing person based on belief that fulfillment will go with him or her...

6. *Difficult to have fun without guilt.*
   - Uncomfortable with being enjoyed and enjoying others.
   - Feel need to be accomplishing something.
   - Difficult to just rest or do nothing.

7. *Have feeling like don't fit in.*
   - Feel out of step with other people and environment.
   - Feel alone and like no one else is or has gone through what you have.

8. *Find it difficult to trust people.*
   - Believe people to be the enemy or the source of pain.
   - Believe each person will harm you as others did.

9. *Feel tired.*
   - Tired of not getting what you want, being down, frustrated, in pain, not getting it, etc. Tired of struggling for something you don't think you'll ever get.

10. *Experience many stress-related illnesses.*
    - Unexplainable illness includes muscle and joint pain, immune system, headaches, etc.

Dream Stealer #5- Performance

11. Tend to code when you communicate.
- You say, "That pizza smells really good!" instead of simply asking for a slice. Assume other will pick up hint without asking directly.
- Intentionally indirect in order to not hurt person or be rejected.
- Afraid to say what you really mean.
- Assume person can and will read your code.

12. Feel overly responsible.
- Believe you have power or ability to make someone happy.
- Feel need to compensate for others' shortcomings or neglect.

13. Have a high level of worry.
- Continually in fear or worry about what others are thinking, doing, feeling.
- Continually second-guessing yourself.

14. A martyr.
- Make excuses for other person's harm.
- Go out of way (expense, work, time, life, etc.) to make other person happy.

- Believe that if you work hard enough, are nice and loving enough, think of other person's feelings instead if your own enough, etc., the person will change or come to finally appreciate and love you.

15. A Victim.
- "I can't," "He won't let me," "She made me," "I will never be able," etc.

16. Afraid of being deserted.
- Feel need to perform or behave in order to hold onto people.
- Being alone equates with failure or unacceptability on your part. ("If I were a better wife, woman, mother, girlfriend, Christian, etc. they would not have left me.")

17. Set inappropriate boundaries.
- Either too relaxed or too rigid. Trying to control pain either way.
- Practicing what you know and experienced.

18. Don't allow mistakes (or admit them).

If you answered YES to 10 or more of the questions, you may have an identity that has a base in low self-esteem, shame or a negative self-concept. If this is you, don't beat yourself up. Many, many people share this with you. The key is to add this information to what we are going to learn about the dream stealer of performance and identify areas that may be holding you back from Dreaming Madly.

PERFORMANCE-BASED IDENTITY

When we think of the word *performance*, we usually relate the word to the arts, work, competition, or something done before an audience. Rarely do we connect the word to our identity; the condition or character as to who we are.

People with a performance-based identity try to get their crucial needs met through what they do instead of who they are. They believe, at some level, that they can earn love, acceptance, and worth by doing something or performing a certain way. They believe that if they can just perform well enough they can control the people and the world around them.

Often people will try to change their character, look different, act different, or will accept bad behavior from someone due to the belief that their performance will earn someone's love. Some will judge others, deny any struggles they have in life, have an arrogant attitude, or appear strong and overly confident. Still others will work hard at their places of employment, positions of leadership, as parents, church members, teachers, CEOs, and students believing the harder they work and sacrifice the higher level of worth they will gain.

Young, old, male, female, positively programmed or negatively programmed, we all struggle with areas of performance-based identity. The reason why comes from the words of Janet Jackson's 1986 hit song, "Control": *"Control of what I say, Control of what I do ... Control to get what I want".*[1]

Performance-based identities are grounded in the desired for control. As humans, we cannot control certain events, God, other people, or the future, and we do not like that. However, if we can somehow hold onto the belief that we have a measure of control in how an event, God, other people, or the future will respond, we feel empowered and in the driver's seat of our own lives.

The difficulty is in realizing that with the exception of a few things, we have very little control in our lives. Even our next breath or knowing if we will return home after saying goodbye to the family in the morning is out of our complete control.

Imagine this scenario: It is Christmas Day and my friend Valecia has a holiday dinner party and invites me. She spends the night before and the morning of cleaning the house and preparing everything for her guests. One of my favorite desserts made by Valecia is her Watergate Salad and she is making an extra bowl just for me. Imagine me entering her house and immediately starting to wipe off counters and clean the floors. Of course, Valecia would ask, "Charlotte, what are you doing? I've already spent the morning cleaning the house." I ignore her and continue cleaning and setting the table. Again, Valecia would ask, "What are you doing?" I reply, "I know you made an extra bowl of Watergate Salad for me, and I just wanted to do something to let you know I'm grateful." Valecia would smile and in her humorous way would say, "I made it so you could enjoy it, not work for it!"

While the scenario is laughable, we do similar performances all the time. It might not be an attempt to earn a way to the Watergate Salad bowl, but other scenarios happen in which we believe we need to earn or perform well in order to receive.

Performance-based identities can be difficult to interpret in our everyday lives. In my 2010 survey, some statements were targeted to show how performance is imbued throughout our lives.

In the survey, eighty-four percent of respondents believed, "People like me because I go out of my way help people." Fifty-three percent believed, "I am a good person because I do good things." Fifty-two percent agreed with the statement, "I give in to things I don't want to do because I don't want to disappoint others." Sixty-eight percent believed, "I have worth because I impact people's lives and try to make a difference." A whopping eighty-seven percent agreed with the statement, "It's difficult to ask for help."

All of those statements are based on receiving worth, love, and acceptance through some type of performance. Even finding difficulty in asking for help is based on fear of having less worth.

Now that we have an insight into how performance affects our lives and decisions, let's begin to explore how performance can steal our dreams. Regardless of the degree to which performance influences our identity, the fact remains that everything is a choice and we have the power to allow our performance to stand in the way of our dreams or to choose differently.

PERFORMANCE-THE DREAM STEALER

Performance-based identities are dream stealers because our dreams and each effort along the journey are based on how well we perform. If we make a mistake or fail in an attempt, we see it as an attack on our performance and a reflection of us. If a book is not selling well in our dream of becoming a national best-selling author, we might shut down and throw our dream to the side because the book is not meeting expectations, which is a reflection on our performance. If situations and difficulties are happening along the way, which they will, and we cannot overcome them easily inside our control, we wonder why goals are unmet despite our best performance.

One of the major ways performance acts as a dream stealer is through self-protection. Self-protection or defense mechanisms place a shield around us to keep pain out. The problem is that while the attempt creates a shield, it pushes out people, growth, and potential as well.

One of those self-protective shields takes the form of walls. Walls are emotional limitations that silently state, "I will only allow you to move to within a certain distance in getting to know me before I push you away or shut down." The wall of protection prevents us from sharing and receiving information relationally, which is vital in walking out the journey. If walls are in place, when the journey becomes harder and the thought of giving up seems easier, no emotional support will be in place to help. The journey will be lonely and self-talk will certainly hinder the dream.

Another self-protective shield is unrealistic expectations. The interesting point about having unrealistic expectations of others is that we often have them of ourselves as well. Daily, we expect situations to happen. We expect our children to be home after school by a certain time, the mail carrier to bring the mail daily, and our favorite television programs to show at their designated time and day. All of those are typical expectations.

However, when typical expectations become unrealistic we can easily get discouraged, frustrated and give up on the dreams and visions we long for. A typical expectation of a friend coming to your house for coffee would be that he or she would arrive on time or close to the time of your appointment. It becomes unrealistic when we expect the friend to ask about our absence at a mutual event and then feel hurt and unseen when they don't.

Unrealistic expectations make assumptions about what we believe should happen. When the expectation is unmet, the reaction is not to reverse or lower the expectation, but to ascribe blame or judgment to ourselves, something, or someone else.

Unrealistic expectations become dream stealers by making assumptions of where and what should be happening during the course of our journey to our dreams. When certain expectations are unmet, we slowly alter or begin to doubt our dream and ability to move toward it. With each unmet expectation comes more discouragement, frustration, stirred-up emotions, and push for performance until at some point we simply say, "It's too hard to dream" and stop moving forward.

MESSAGES EXERCISE

We have a final section to complete in our "Messages of the Past" diagram on Page 187. We will be working with the bottom portion of the diagram called "Dream Stealers." In this section, we will begin to make some connections between feelings, emotions, and beliefs we have to dream stealers that we are facing in our journey.

Under the area where you have listed two people, begin to write down any of the dream stealers we have covered and the specific areas of frustration and struggle you find in moving toward your dreams. Write down as many dream stealers and areas of struggle you can think of on the lines under the people column. When you are finished, go to the situation column, do the same, and follow with the "words said" column.

After you complete the diagram return to this page and read further to interpret the meaning of the diagram.

MAKING A CONNECTION

The first section of the diagram reveals the people and situations that have most influenced us. More than likely, the people, situations, and words listed are still playing a role in our lives today in either a negative or a positive way. The first section gives a hint to the main characters and events in our lives and may hold a clue to reasons why moving forward or forgiveness is difficult.

The second section of the diagram reveals the feelings and emotions we have attached to the previous sections. Feelings and emotions eventually become beliefs and filters over time. The longer we hold onto an emotion without further information or a context, the deeper the belief becomes to a point of being fact in our minds.

The third and bottom section of the diagram reveals the ways that we choose to make our lives work to deal with the pain and fears of life. The bottom section reflects the ways we try to get our crucial needs (love, acceptance, and worth) met from other people and things, instead of through who we are.

The purpose of the "Messages of the Past" diagram is to demonstrate how messages we received from the past and through our lives have formed certain belief systems, emotions, and filters. In turn, those belief systems, emotions, and filters alter the way we view the world around us and in most cases created behaviors, habits, and defenses to make our lives work for us.

In the process, dream stealers and attempts to make our lives safer, easier, and more comfortable replaced the freedom and creativity of our childhood. In order to begin to Dream Madly, Pursue Wildly and Trust Completely and return to a place of freedom and creativity, those dream stealers and attempts have to be addressed.

The great news is that we always have the opportunity to change, make new choices, take a different path, or begin again. Becoming aware of our frailties, wounds, and imperfections never disqualifies us from our dreams. Instead, they are part of the story that plays out in our lives toward reaching the dream.

Performance, our emotions, fears, other people, or the past do not bind our dreams. The journey is not about becoming a better dreamer, dreaming with perfection or being strong and never failing. The journey to Dreaming Madly is the opposite. It is understanding, guarding, and learning as much as we can in preparation for the journey ahead while, like a child in its father's arms, is resting, staying in the moment, and allowing herself to be who she is while dreaming.

CHAPTER TEN

PURSUING WILDLY: THE JOURNEY FEARED

"The unexamined life is not worth living for a human being."

---- **Socrates** (469 BC–399 BC)

Often, we will have a dream in our heart, a business we want to start, an idea we desire to invent, a book we need to write, or a vision we have been given that stirs in our heart, but we fail to move forward because we lack direction. The longer we lack direction without seeking help to reach it, the sooner that dream or vision moves to the back of our minds and ends up as a mere memory.

If we don't add action to our thoughts and plans they simply become great conversation pieces of the future, of the times when we say, "Well, you know, once I had an idea to…" Direction can become an excuse because we can easily blame our failure to succeed on "I didn't have anyone to help me" or "I just didn't know how to do it." Let's be clear: EVERYTHING is a choice.

The real obstacle with direction is not the lack of information or resources, but the humility and courage needed in asking for help. Whoever believes or states to others, "I am a self-made _____" is lying. It is impossible to succeed or move toward our dreams and visions without soliciting the help of others.

The easiest part of dreaming is having a dream. Yes, it takes time for the mind to allow itself to explore its imagination and push past the self-limiting boundaries of current reality. However, dreaming is fun, wild, challenging and only requires our willingness to free our minds and move toward what we have been called to be. Dreaming is the easy part.

Walking out the journey toward our dreams, now that is downright difficult. Actually, the greatest war and the most battles are lost during the process of walking out the journey of traveling toward our dreams. The journey is where we either build our character or lose hope. It is where we become stronger, bolder, and yield ourselves to become someone we could be or we retreat to the unsettling safety of being common, ordinary, unchallenged, and short of our potential.

The journey prepares and defines who we are, why we dream, and why we are the only ones who can complete it. In short, the dream is important, but the dream has no meaning and little importance without the wealth that is gained from the process of the journey. All too often, we begin excited and motivated, believing that in only a few weeks, months or perhaps years, our dreams will come into fruition with just a few hiccups, obstacles, or setbacks.

Time passes and we begin to doubt our ability to pursue our dreams and ourselves. We become discouraged because the dream is not happening as fast or the way we thought it would happen. People start to ask about the length of time it is taking our dream to come true. We begin to remember past failures or words, then gradually slow our walk until we stand still.

PURSUING WILDLY

What does it mean to Pursue Wildly? It means to explore every avenue, open every door, and ask every question you can, challenge your feelings, push away dream killers, and pursue your course of action as though your life depended on it.

When I decided to write my first book, I was clueless. I knew what a book looked like and where they were sold but beyond much more than that, I had no idea about the business, marketing, writing, formatting, or anything. Before that book went to market a year and a half later, I felt like I had given birth. I researched everything from how to format a book, write a book, phrasing, creating book covers, and book sizes to reading everything I could on marketing, promotion, publicity, publishers, and creating book trailers. I talked and asked questions of anybody in the industry who would talk with me and offered to buy lunch with top executives of publishing companies to gain wisdom about the business and marketing. I think you get the point.

Understanding the "Pursuing Wildly" part is easy. The question is are you willing to do it? To Dream Madly means we have to take a risk to dream while closing our minds to the obstacles, emotions, and circumstances that are in the way. To Pursue Wildly means we have to take a risk to believe in our dream and ourselves enough to close our mind to the dream killers, discouragement, difficultly and waiting that will get in our way during the journey. It is a journey of courage. That is Pursuing Wildly!

ONE MAN'S SIMPLE DREAM

Jack Kavanagh was a wild dreamer who showed obstacles like age, great responsibility, and limitations can never stand in the way of our dreams. Carl Brashear was a wild dreamer who proved no dream stealer, not even handicap, could ever steal someone's dreams.

I would like to tell you about another wild dreamer. He did not dream about being a writer, a leader, a person of position, about having wealth or fame, or even about accomplishing great things according to the world's view. He had a simple dream of one day having a family and making a better life for them than he had. He was a dreamer who knew a dream has no requirements or stipulations in order to be a great dream. It simply had to be your dream, even a simple dream.

My grandfather, Rufus Malone, was a stoic, hardworking, "I show love by providing for you, not by saying it," disciplinarian type of man while his wife was the epitome of big hugs, home cooking, and tender touches of love. Despite his rough exterior, one of the greatest qualities I remember about him was that he was a dreamer.

He was born in 1899 and came from a generation of hardworking, proud people who daily stared reality in the face. His life was incredibly hard. My grandfather's parents were the first generation out of slavery and he carried the baggage of prejudice, injustice, and oppression on his shoulders like a huge unpaid debt.

When my grandfather was old enough to leave his home in Georgia, he set a dream in place. It was a simple dream but one that he pursued as though his life depended on accomplishing that dream. He had a dream to live "up north," as he called it, and to make a better life for himself. He dreamed of one day having a family that would have an easier life than he did. It was a simple dream of hope and a plan for the future. It was a dream that my grandfather knew would cost a great deal to pursue. However, like a child who is blind to the doubts of others, my grandfather Dreamed Madly.

In his time, airplanes and taxis were not available and certainly were not welcomed to a man of color. My grandfather had no money to afford one of Henry Ford's Model T cars so he simply walked. He walked and hitchhiked, hoping to land a ride from friendly strangers for a few miles north. He slept in fields, worked for food and a bed for the night in someone's barn or back room, then walked some more to move inch by inch toward his determined dream.

My grandfather told me stories of being arrested for vagrancy, having to run for his life from the Ku Klux Klan, and going to sleep many nights without having eaten. He described the aches and pains of his body and constant bleeding of his feet due to blisters and calluses. There was a cost, but my grandfather had a dream.

Eventually, my grandfather landed in Akron, Ohio, and found work in one of the rubber factories. In time, he married and had a son and three daughters. He became a church leader and elder, friend, and beloved man until his death in 1996 of Lou Gehrig's disease. Over his life, his dream came into fruition. He made a better life for himself and had a family who highly valued education, hard work, fortitude and a desire to dream and be more than the word "normal" required.

My grandfather was far from being a perfect man. He was uncomfortable with the show of affection, heavy-handed with discipline, and firm in his beliefs regarding society and morality. However, he was a man of determination, drive, and passion, and was steadfast in dreaming and pursuing his dreams for himself and his children regardless of the cost.

My grandfather was my first introduction to the word and the work of dreaming. I absolutely loved my both of my grandparents and often wanted to stay in the comfort of their home, where I could run, play, be myself, and allow my imagination to run free. They helped me to realize that the world was so much bigger than the reality of my circumstances, feelings, or beliefs. Although events and dream stealers would invade my life, my grandparents' foundation helped me to return to the realization that nothing could ever thwart me from my dreams outside of death or myself. My grandfather's simple dream is his legacy that lives on through everyone's path I cross and through me.

BEGINNING A JOURNEY- SAFE PLACE/PEOPLE

In Chapter One, I asked some questions. I asked, "When was the last time you allowed yourself to dream like a child? When was the last time you allowed yourself to escape from the believed boundaries, limitations, situations, and stresses in your life long enough to ask, 'What if?'"

The journey starts by going back to the beginning-- the place where we feel a sense of safety and rest and are able to do nothing but allow our minds to wander and stretch to the farthest corners of our imagination. We need to return to that childlike place where the only limitations to our dreams are the limitations of our imagination.

To this point, I have used the example of a father's arms to represent a place of safety where a little boy or girl opens up their world of imagination and dreams to explore what they want to be when they grow up. That example is not by accident. There is something about the strength and safety of a father's arms that offers a comfort and message that no other place can give.

We want to be able to relax and shake off the made-up rules that said we were wrong to play and laugh and dream aloud.

We want to recall that time when we were safe in our daddy's arms, all that mattered was then, and we could dream and be anything and everything. We were not childish, we were childlike and had more wisdom and freedom than any well-educated adult had.

The place of a father's arms is not so much literal as figurative. It is necessary to recall the feeling of being in our father's arms or at least a place of safety and rest to begin to recapture some of the freedom of being childlike. It is a place where we can say what we want and be who we are without judgment, criticism, or limitation.

A mother's arms provide love and nurture but are not the first thing that comes to mind when longing for strength and power. A brother or sister's arms provide love and comfort but are not the first things that come to mind when longing for protection and rest. A father's arms represent a mixture of tenderness, protection, leadership, strength, comfort, and rest needed for the dreamer's journey.

Maybe you can recall being in the strong and safe arms of your father and remember the long-lost dreams of your childhood. For some, that place of freedom and safety was not in a father's arms but in the arms of a loving mother while in the nursery. For some, that place may have been with a stepparent, grandparent or relative who offered care, love and safety.

Still, for some like me, trying to recall a place of safety, love, or even a place of protection where dreams and imagination could run free is a difficult, if not disturbing, task. A father might represent danger, damage or a lack of protection.

For some, a father's arms will be too hard to grasp and it will be more trying than helpful in moving toward dreams. If that is the case, use a person who represents safety, rest, freedom, and joy. Imagine a grandmother's or a father type figure's arms. It will need to be someone who can respond and interact.

For men especially, this return might be difficult not only due to any past issues but also because of a society that wrongly places judgments on demonstrations of tenderness from men. If it is more comfortable, choose a female that represents tenderness and safety for you.

Returning to a place and setting of freedom and imagination is vital in learning to Dream Madly. However, what can one do to move forward when finding that place is difficult? One can do what others who have overcome situations and obstacles have done in order to move forward: create a new place of memories.

I did not have the safe and loving arms of a father who asked me what I wanted to be when I grew up, so in order to begin to dream again, I had to create that place.

There is no place like a father's arms. Regardless of how good or bad a father is in reality, the design of who he is meant to be and the role he is meant to serve have no greater place. It is envisioning sitting on the lap of a father who simply loves and enjoys us for us. We don't have to perform, earn the right to be on his lap, limit our time on his lap, or feel foolish for any dream no matter how large or small.

The more we focus on that place of safety and rest and connection, the more freedom we will have in recalling dreams that are locked away and begin dreaming new dreams birthing inside us.

Along with finding a safe place to return to mentally in pursuing the journey, we also need to find safe people. We need to walk with safe people during our journey who will tell us the truth and offer feedback while encouraging us to dream further.

Safe people are those who ask questions and make suggestions to exhort us to be and do more. They take risks to ask hard questions and remain engaged in the relationship in the midst of conflict and disappointment. Importantly, they hold our secrets, personal details, and vulnerabilities and dreams valuable and confidential and allow us to be who we are in the midst of our imperfections. That is a safe person.

WRITE IT DOWN

Daily I mentor or speak with people who have incredible ideas and dreams. They have a passion and a great desire to bring their dreams to fruition. However, when I ask them, "So what is your next move?" or "What is your plan to make it happen?" Eight out of ten times the person is clueless or never considered a game plan.

For those of us who are planners and administrators, we love to plan, create sticky notes, make lists, and make sticky notes of the things on lists that we want to accomplish for that day. For everyone else, the thought of putting together a plan, researching avenues, making connections, getting organized and working a plan are one step worse than going to the dentist.

Most people don't like the administration side of walking out their dream. If planning is not your strength, find help. Ask others who have moved forward on their dreams to make suggestions or work with you. The key is beginning to write out the long-term dream/vision and the process of steps in between to reach that dream.

Begin by writing down your dream. Write as much detail as possible regarding your dream. If tomorrow every detail of your wildest dream could come true, what would it look like? What are the things or situations you dream about that cause you to lose time or take you to another place? What is the dream or the vision that stirs inside of you and gives you new energy when you begin to imagine the possibilities?

As you ponder your dream, think about the details. Will you be living in your present location or somewhere else? Are other people involved directly in your dream or are you the primary character? How will your life change? Will you have a family, be travelling, living in a large house, living overseas, making a large income, volunteering, running a home, or leading on a global level? How many people will the organization, ministry, or company employ? Who will be your audience, client base, or ministry to serve?

Write every detail of your dream, then begin to work backward and think of the small steps needed to help the bigger dream come true. This part will be tricky. Keep in mind we are Dreaming Madly and dreaming dreams big enough to fail. Writing out the steps is a guideline, not a promised destination point. Remember, many things are out of our control and won't submit to our agenda simply because we had a plan. However, if we do not put a road map and smaller steps in place, it will be easy to feel overwhelmed by the size of the dream and get discouraged when we can't see our way.

THINK LIKE A BUSINESSPERSON

Once you have a written plan for how you're going to proceed, think like a businessperson instead of an individual with a wonderful dream. I remember watching a television program where inventors or people who had ideas and dreams could present them to judges who would give them money based on the quality of their idea. That show proved my point. The contestants who usually received money by the end of the show were those who had a plan worked out, done the needed research, had a great product or vision to accomplish it and thought in terms of business. Others who seemed to lack the business sense and approach did not fare as well.

Become an expert in your area of pursuit. If you want to begin a non-profit to provide cosmetics or health and beauty advice to women in underprivileged countries, become an expert as you pursue it. Learn and understand the psychology of self-image and the cultural norms of the women you're serving. How much is your non-profit going to need? Who will be your supplier of goods to the women? Your dream becomes a type of business the moment you include other people in it.

Understand your audience for the dream you plan to pursue. For example, let's say you have a dream of becoming a national speaker and affecting people's lives. If you have difficulty communicating clearly, perhaps vocal training will help or the dream altered based on your ability. Again, go beyond the passion of what you want to do and think in a business-like way of realizing what you need to make that dream happen.

UNDERSTANDING THE COST

Recently, some plans I had hoped to come through failed within a twenty-four hour period. I was crushed. So much of what I had hoped for and relied on was based on my plan coming to fruition. Somehow in the turn and tide of the universe, the world did not sway to my organization, rules, knowhow and control. How dare they?

A day that started out as hopeful and exciting ended up as sad, miserable and lonely. In my pain, I did what other people who teach about leadership and following dreams did ... I cried, threw a tantrum, felt sorry for myself, got into bed to wash away my sorrows in the escape of a *Criminal Minds* marathon on television and ate my favorite foods of chicken fingers, French fries, and a lemonade with a pint of Haagen-Dazs® ice cream as a chaser.

I would love to tell you that the bullets and arrows of setbacks and situations that seem to move us away from dreams instead of toward dreams do not penetrate my cape of Dreaming Madly, Pursuing Wildly, and Trusting Completely, but they do.

I am not writing this to discourage you but to encourage you to know that part of the deal in Dreaming Madly is understanding the cost. It is understanding that there will be times, like I had, when you want to chuck it all and say, "Forget it; I want to be like everybody else and just be normal!"

Through the journey of Pursuing Wildly there will be times when you will doubt yourself and believe you have lost your senses. You will believe everyone who has ever told you to grow up, be normal and stop dreaming, "get a life," "do what everybody else is doing," "get a real job," or has asked, "Why can't you be like everybody else?" "Isn't it time to put your dream aside and come into the real world?" and everything else said over what you know in your heart. You will feel like you are the biggest failure on earth because others seem to be "doing" while you are dreaming and trusting. You will be in a path of a few viewing a field of many because you have chosen the path less taken, and it will be difficult.

In my time of hurt and frustration, I found myself yelling over and over again, "I just want to be normal and stop being a dreamer, stop wanting more!" Even as I write that statement out, it seems crazy. Not crazy that I would want to stop being a dreamer because I understand the pain of hoping for something that may never happen the way I want it to happen. What is crazy in hindsight is that I would desire to stop wanting more.

BE THE EXCEPTION, NOT THE RULE

Many people will get excited or motivated by something that is said or done. Then, depending on the person, many will fail to move forward because the road to their dreams is not easier, wider, faster, less costly or in reach. In time, they will get tired and burned out, then eventually lessen their dream to something more compatible with their comfort zone. They will remain in the number of those who had big dreams but never pursued them.

No one should work harder or care more about our dreams than we do. If our dreams and visions are not worth moving out of our comfort zone, learning a new skill, or growing as a person in the process, perhaps it is not a dream worth following.

It is easy to look at a Donald Trump, a Beth Moore, an Oprah Winfrey, or a John Maxwell and marvel at their accomplishments and the dreams and goals they set for themselves and achieved. If you ask every one of them, they will tell you stories of the labor that came with those visions and dreams and how every step was worth it.

There is no such thing as coincidence. Your vision is yours. Your dream is yours. You are the one who has been assigned for the task. Please do not allow life, your past, feelings, obstacles, dream killers, or yourself to get in the way of that dream. You CAN do this.

CHAPTER ELEVEN

TRUSTING COMPLETELY: THE WAITING GAME

"To be trusted is a greater compliment than to be loved."

---- George MacDonald, *The Marquis of Lossie* (1877), Chapter IV.

Dreaming Madly requires us to stretch our imagination to its fullest. Pursuing Wildly requires us to walk a journey of perseverance into the unknown. Trusting Completely requires faith and vulnerability. By definition, the word "trust" means, "To hope or expect confidently." 1

Unlike the first two processes, trusting is an action of being, not doing, and is the simplest of the three yet the hardest to live out.

What does it mean to Trust Completely? It means to believe that not only is our dream worth having but also we are worth having a dream that is big and great enough to fail! There is no greater dream worth pursuing in life.

Trusting is being on our last tank of oxygen while nearing the top of Mt. Everest. We are not sure if we are going to reach the top because of knowing others have fallen behind or quit. We want to give up but know there is no turning back because we know and we have faith that we are destined to reach the top.

To Trust Completely does not mean we will have a guarantee that whatever we Deam Madly and Pursue Wildly will happen. It's just not that easy. If we dreamed big enough, more than likely we will have failure in our pursuit. If there is no failure, there is no growth, no learning.

Yeah, I got a great finished product with my first book, but it took nine drafts and two complete story changes before I got it right and understood what I truly needed to say. I would not change a thing because of the invaluable information and experiences I gained in the process of writing that book.

Trusting Completely is not about getting it right, it's about getting *us* right. It is about growing and changing in the process forever. If our first attempt falls short, we can still move forward, change routes, and then push further. If we found the dream needed altering, we can change the dream, reorganize, and then push forward. Too many people get to the top of the hill, hit a bump in the road, and then throw everything to the wind believing the best route is to give up.

The best route is to take a TV timeout, breathe, and get back to work. If the dream or goal is easy, it is not worth having. We were born to be more. We were born to have a commitment to a dream and walk it out. If trusting were easy, more evidence of greatness would exist in our society.

To Trust Completely means we have to take a risk that our life was meant for more than we believe it to be. Our dreams and visions are in place as part of our purpose to fulfill our potential and possibilities. While we can hold no one accountable for holding us back, we also can hold no one or nothing accountable for preventing us from moving forward.

Trusting Completely is not handing ourselves over to a blind trust for the sake of affecting others. It is first trusting that we are the only ones who can do and answer the dream or vision we have been given. It is trusting that our dream is not a mere wish or something someone else can accomplish. A dream, hope, or vision that is simple or can be done by anyone does not require the depth of pursuing, dreaming, and trust we are discussing in this book.

Trusting Completely is certainly about the dream and the process. However, the most important piece is to trust that we are the only ones to answer our dream. Our dreams are attached to who we are. Mahatma Gandhi, Martin Luther King, and the Wright Brothers each had a dream. In 2005 Steve Chen, Chad Hurley, and Jawed Karim had a dream for an online video sharing and viewing community. It became YouTube. They had one thing in common: They trusted in their dreams completely.

FAITH VERSUS TRUST

It is impossible to discuss the word "trust" without also dealing with the word "faith." We are using "trust" as a verb, an action word of walking in the process of hoping and confidently expecting a certain outcome to happen regarding our dreams and our future. "Faith" is a noun, a steadfast belief in something for which there is no proof. It is complete trust. Trust and faith both require hope in something for a time that has not happened yet.

Before we can trust for something, we must first have faith in something.

For some, other avenues will be appealing in understanding faith. The best way I can explain the prerequisite of faith to Trusting Completely is to use an example of my personal faith relationship with Christ. My example is not to preach or evangelize. I hope that my life lived out does that. My example is simply to give the best explanation I know to demonstrate how impossible it is to trust without first having faith.

In the previous chapter, I mentioned plans that failed to come through within a twenty-four hour period in discussing understanding the cost of the journey. The details I left out were that on that day not only was my car and all my money taken, but I had no money to pay for another week at the extended-stay hotel where I was dwelling while looking for a home.

I was two weeks behind writing deadline due to continual distractions and interruptions regarding the book and had recently moved to a new state based on the leading (trust) of my convictions and wise counsel. I was stranded, broke, carless, about to be evicted, desperate, in a new city, alone, and doubting the purpose of my life as well as the hope of any dream. My trust greatly wavered to a point of wanting to give up.

For years, I had known struggle and disruption. My journey of trusting and living moment to moment for the many dreams and destinations placed in my life was not foreign to me.

However, on that day, I had nothing left. The preceding week of disappointments left me weary.

In the two hours between the theft events and the deadline to hotel checkout, I made it through because of one thing – faith. Above trusting that God would come through and rescue me from the situation, in whatever way that would happen, I relied on faith in Him. My trust is hopeful and confident that He will come through for me. However, my faith first acknowledges that He is able to do what He says He can do. Before I can trust and confidently expect He will do something, I have to believe He is able to make it happen.

Similarly, in a human relationship, before we can trust that a person will keep our secrets and walk safely in our lives, we must have a measure of faith and belief in their unproven character that they are able to be that type of friend.

Faith is vital because there will be times in the journey when the going will be rough, our hope will sway, and our confidence in expecting an outcome to happen will sag. Our trust will be tested. Faith, unlike trust, is steadfast and does not change because of struggles or situations. Either we believe in something for which there is no proof, whatever that might be, or we don't.

The key for each of us will be to find something we can have faith in that is bigger than we are as we pursue our dreams. We will need a source to cling to when the journey gets rough and trusting is hard. Keep in mind, if the subject of our faith is faulty, our trust will be weak.

By the way, an hour before time to check out from the hotel, the manager called my room to say someone had anonymously paid another week's stay for me. To this day, I have no idea who that person was. Each day miracles happen, a new dream grows, and so my faith continues and trust grows stronger.

WHAT DOES TRUSTING LOOK LIKE?

Trusting is the opposite of worry. When we trust someone with handling a task for us, we are not micromanaging his or her actions, fearing the task will not be completed, or worried when they will finish the task. We know beyond any doubt that person will get the task done and do what is required. If we do not trust that person, we are in constant worry, checking on the person's progress, and fearing the completion of the task, as we desire.

When we trust, we are at rest. Although we are concerned about the result, we can rest in knowing the process is moving us forward and the result will take place regardless of the timing, journey, or the events we experience.

Trusting Completely for our dreams is the same. When we trust in our dream completely, we are able to do all of the actions we are responsible to do and regardless of the timing, the bumps and turns of the journey, and the difficult situations we might face, we know that at some point, our dream will take place.

Trusting is difficult because we want to see our dream happen in our timing and in the way we expect and that rarely is the situation. In order to trust completely, we have to release our dream to the process of time and at the risk of failing or a change of direction.

THE TRUTH ABOUT TRUST

1. **Trust is the opposite of control.** Trust is not willing something to happen, controlling something, or focusing on the object. To trust in our dream means that we do every possible thing we can to assist in bringing the dream to fruition, then trust in the process and the journey.

2. **Trust is not a one-time commitment, it is a daily choice.**

3. **Trust in a dream does not mean that the journey will be smooth or pain-free.**

4. **The greatest opponent to trust is fear.** The dance goes like this. A dream or vision beats in our heart and we hear it calling. We become excited and imagine new possibilities and begin planning and pursuing. Others encourage us and we have moments of success and hope for a future dream.

Time passes, situations don't go as planned, the dream is not falling into place as easily as we expected, money is running low, others seem to pass us by in success, we doubt and become afraid, and then we stop trusting. It is a dance we play over the course of walking out any pursuit of greatness.

5. **Trust is learned and acquired**. Trust is learned through the process of trusting more. As babies and children, we naturally trust. Through the disappointments of life we learn that trust is for the foolish. The way we gradually learn to trust again is by taking the risk to trust. We cannot buy it, earn it or hope for it. We learn how to trust by trusting at greater levels, which means allowing ourselves to take greater risks of vulnerability.

6. **Trusting is NEVER the problem, although the source may be**. Often we make a decision to put up a wall due to past hurts or betrayals of our trust. Out of our hurt, we decide that we will never trust again. The problem was not that we trusted. Trusting is a normal and healthy act. The problem we often have is the source in which we place our trust. Unfortunately, due to our hurt we confused the two and protect ourselves, not realizing we are actually doing the opposite.

7. **There is a difference between trusting in something and trusting for something.** To trust in our dream means that we

believe that regardless of the journey, the direction the dream takes, or the fruition of the dream, it is worth having and worth fighting for. To trust for our dream means that we believe that our dream must happen exactly how we imagined and planned it without fail. Trusting for our dream keeps the focus solely on the dream and making it happen no matter what. The purpose alone is seeing the dream as a goal to be met.

My hope is that we are trusting in our dreams and the pursuit of them. In doing so, the process is about more than a mere dream. It about growing, being changed, going beyond ordinary and stretching ourselves to our potential in finding possibilities and our impact in the world around us, all while moving toward our dream. The focus is the dream but the destination is moving toward a life that matters and making a difference in whatever way that appears.

WAITING GAME -- AN ACHE OF TRUSTING

It seems easy to ask others to trust and to Trust Completely. The fact remains, trusting is incredibly difficult, and for many of us, it is something we fear. We fear because of past hurts, betrayals and misuses of our trust. Somewhere along the way we consciously or subconsciously yelled, "I will never trust like that again!" As with the messages of our past, we gained another belief and put up another wall in the effort to keep pain out and safety in.

Unfortunately, our dreams can't and never will operate only inside safe walls. Our dreams require the help and participation of others. They place us in a position where we have to trust others and learn how to trust in the process along the way. Those dreams and the journey in moving toward those dreams call for us to learn how to wisely trust and leave the life of safety and the known in spite of our fears.

Part of Trusting Completely is being in the waiting room. One of the most difficult processes in the journey is waiting. We all will experience a time when it feels as though time is standing still and nothing is being accomplished. Often we will be tempted to start working harder or trying something different in order to inject life into our dying dream.

The fact is our dreams are not dying at all. We are simply in a normal process in the journey called waiting. Despite our efforts, we can't make the dream happen faster. We hate it because "hope deferred makes the heart grow sick" (Proverbs 13:12)

When we are waiting, all of our attention is focused on the result of that thing. However, when we are focused on the dream instead of the missed deadline, money problems, and delays, things seem to happen unexpectedly and sometimes very quickly.

The best use of time in the waiting room is to trust that the process is happening regardless of sight and situations and to trust that a dream is meant to be and is taking place regardless of what is happening.

THE LIES WE BELIEVE WHILE WE WAIT

Over the course of this book, I have made reference to a survey I conducted in 2010 of sixty questions. A sample of the 2010 survey is on Page 193. I was alarmed by the results of the survey and the degree of hopelessness, false beliefs and lies that were reflected. The results of that survey prompted me to begin to research and write regarding our dreams and potential, and the idea of pursuing and trusting that our lives mattered and made a difference.

Here are some of the results from the survey to assist in recognizing fact from fiction. The numbers represent the percentage of people that stated "yes" with the statements.

Lies we believe about ourselves
1. I'm a good person because I do good things. - **53%**
2. I need things to go my way to be happy and content. - **78%**
3. Others don't (clean, organize, handle situations, etc.) like I can so I need to do it to make sure it's right. - **53%**
4. When I am hurt or disappointed I feel I need to do something, eat or take something to feel better. - **52%**
5. I would be okay if abuse never happened. - **50%**
6. I have worth because I impact people's lives and try to make a difference. - **68%**
7. It is hard for me to have guilt-free fun or totally relax. - **55%**

8. It's better to hold in my emotions and anger than to let it all out. - **57%**
9. If I don't do it, it won't be done. - **58%**
10. Things will get better if I try harder. - **84%**
11. I take things personally. - **71%**
12. The problem is that I just need to have more faith (in whatever it may be). - **45%**
13. I have unexplainable illnesses (i.e. headaches, stomach aches, etc.) that are not connected to a known disease that I have. - **13%**
14. I'm over my issues because I'm older or feel better. - **58%**
15. I usually feel that something is wrong with me.– **58%**
16. I need to keep my eyes on my goal instead of enjoying the journey. - **53%**
17. I can't be of great use unless I have it together and am strong. - **39%**
18. When I am not moving forward or my life is not working, I get sad, angry or depressed. - **74%**
19. I need to use code to communicate. (Drop hints to get someone to do something or react) - **32%**
20. I get hurt easily. - **61%**
21. If I were doing things right, my life would be going better and I would not have struggles like I do. - **35%**
22. I am successful because I have accomplished a lot. - **16%**
23. I am a bad person because I do bad things. - **16%**
24. I worry about things all the time. - **58%**

25. I often react based on how I feel. - **68%**
26. It is better to be strong than vulnerable. - **94%**
27. I am not successful, a good person, able to achieve great things, etc. because of my past or failures in my past. - **26%**
28. I am afraid of being abandoned by people. - **52%**
29. It's easy for me to find fault with myself and/or others. - **74%**
30. I can't forgive people who have harmed me greatly. - **61%**
31. I don't feel attractive unless I look like a model. – **50%**
32. I have no choice in the matter. - **88%**
33. I need to use my sexuality or looks to be acceptable. - **45%**
34. Crying, being vulnerable and talking to people about my problems are signs of weakness. - **42%**

Lies we believe about others

1. I can't trust people because I'll get hurt. - **63%**
2. Life would be better if I had a significant other. - **67%**
3. I set very high standards and expectations for myself. - **84%**
4. I am unhappy because of someone else in my life or my past. - **65%**
5. People can't handle the real me. - **52%**
6. I offer advice to others to help them, even if they don't ask. - **33%**
7. I will never allow myself to get hurt like that again. - **61%**
8. I am afraid to confront people who I think will reject me. - **61%**
9. I need to keep a wall up to protect myself. - **50%**

10. When I'm in a romantic relationship, I am usually the one taking charge. – **38%**
11. It's difficult to ask for help. - **87%**
12. I get jealous of others' happiness. - **55%**
13. I give in to things I don't want to do because I don't want to disappoint others. - **52%**
14. People like me because I go out of my way to help. - **84%**
15. It is easy for me to get obsessive about things or people. - **39%**
16. People can make me happy or sad. - **100%**
17. If people really knew me, they would abandon or reject me. - **30%**
18. I need love and acceptance from people. - **68%**
19. I need to meet the emotional needs of others. - **58%**

Lies we believe about the world around us
1. Life should be fair. - **52%**
2. Either something is right or it is wrong. Either someone is good or they are bad. - **53%**

In the course of walking out our dreams, fighting off dream stealers, and being in the waiting room, we believe lies and false beliefs and filters that cut off potential. The bad news is that each of the above statements represents a lie or false belief that stemmed from a distorted or misplaced message that can compromise our trust, especially in the waiting room. The good news is that each lie and false belief can change through grasping the truth, professional help if needed, and time.

On Page 197 is a sheet called "Reminders of the Truth" that will be helpful to read in those questioning moments in the waiting room.

CHAPTER TWELVE

A DREAM FROM YOUR STORY

"Life is not measured by the number of breaths we take, but by the moments that take our breath away."

---- **Claimed by Erica Frandsen in Kochmer, Casey; Erica Frandsen (2002)**

One of my favorite movies is *Saving Private Ryan*. Although the opening scenes are horribly sobering to watch, the movie shows the horror of war and the honor of sacrifice in a way that only the talent of a Steven Spielberg can capture. My respect for the military and veterans of previous wars grew a hundredfold after watching it.

Many scenes stood out for me as poignant. However, one not only brought tears to my eyes but also beautifully stated what we are all to do with our stories.

Captain John H. Miller, played by Tom Hanks, has traveled a long and dangerous journey with his men through battle to find the last remaining son of a grieved mother. Most of his men have died or been wounded in the process of trying to save Private James Ryan, played by Matt Damon.

Captain Miller has suffered a mortal wound and is offering his last words to the man for whom he and his team have sacrificed. In his last breath Captain Miller looks into Private Ryan's eyes and says, *"James ... earn this. Earn it."*[1] Even as I write and recall that moment in the movie, chills run up my arms. Those few words say it all. Captain Miller was asking James Ryan to earn the sacrifice and the journey that happened on his behalf.

The captain did not ask him to pay the sacrifice forward but to earn the sacrifice and the story of what happened on that day.

The journey of the stories of our lives is no different. Regardless of the pain, losses, joys, trials and intersections, our stories are not to merely be lived or even paid forward, but to be earned and used for a purpose.

A STORY'S PURPOSE

Our stories are a combination of the people, places, things, situations, circumstances, experiences, feelings, and actions of our beginnings to this point. Like the telling of a good novel, our stories have a beginning, a development of characters, a time when life was easy and good, a time of difficulty or obstacles to overcome, a journey of discovery and survival, and a resolution or resolve toward the future. We all have a story; it simply looks different for each of our lives.

Our stories include the burdens, passions, and themes of our lives that offer hints to our purpose, possibilities and potential and act as the foundation for our dreams. As a beautiful painting needs a particular type of frame, so our dreams require the stories that are woven into our lives.

A purpose lies in our stories. Something is meant to happen because of them. Our stories should cause us to look back, learn, and make changes for our future. We can go back and learn from the great things we have done, the wrong choices, the pain, those moments when we said, "Never again!," the places where we went left instead of right, and those things we responded to because we were hurting.

Our stories should give us hope. What is hope? Hope is remembering the events of the past and recalling the joys, dreams and visions while eagerly anticipating their fulfillment in a time that hasn't occurred yet.

Our stories show us our wiring and our uniqueness. There are a zillion people in the world but each of us has a unique story. You have a unique story, certain pain, and struggles you have gone through, talents, thoughts, gifts, abilities that only you can bring to the table to make a difference or impact in someone's life.

Our stories, as long as we are honest with ourselves, are always true. No one can say our story is a lie, is not the right type of story, or we don't have a story ... because it's our story. No one can say it didn't happen. No one can say that wasn't a good story or the right story. No one can compare stories, because each one is unique and designed to be lived by that person.

Often we believe our stories have less value or impact because they lack the drama of someone who has an abused, addicted, or traumatic past. We discount our stories because our lives do not contain tales of survival or life-changing events. That's not true at all. The stories we have are the stories we have. My life is no more important or special because I had a past of abuse, addiction, and tragedy than someone who had a picture-perfect past. The only difference between my story and anyone else's is the particular events of my story have an attachment to my particular purpose. The particular events of your story have an attachment to the particular purpose in your life.

Finally, our stories bring change to our piece of the world and can impact lives. In other words, our stories should not keep us stuck in the past or be used to sing the constant chorus of "Nobody knows da trouble I've seen." Our stories are the only thing we have and can give away that offers our lives meaning.

READING YOUR STORY

Before we can begin to write, tell, and use our stories, we need to know how to read our stories. A wonderful guide for reading our stories is an understanding of our passions, burdens, and the reoccurrences of our lives. These three areas are vital in connecting our stories with dreams and purposes in our lives. If we don't know how to read our story, we won't know how to use our story.

What are our passions? The word "passion" has a few different meanings. It means an *"ardent affection for an activity, object, or concept"*2 such as having a passion for music, animals, conservation. The definition we are focusing on is *"an intense, driving, overmastering feeling or conviction,"*3 such as a passion to influence, encourage, help, write, etc. In general, our passions reflect the actions or methods by which we share our burdens. Our passions are action words and the ways we love to move in others' lives and how we communicate our burden. They are actions we love but will be for others.

What are our burdens? The word "burden" is much deeper than passion. It is something that we carry, a duty, a responsibility. While burdens are often thought of in the negative sense, in the case of our stories, they are positive. Our burden is something that we must do, tell, reach out to, impress upon others, and fight for, etc., because of our story.

It's a good thing. Our burden is the thing that if asked, we could talk about passionately for hours. It is more than a cause; it is a part of us. In other words, if we only had one day to live and had a platform to speak to the entire world for five minutes, what would be the one thing we would want them to know? That is our burden. In general, our burdens are about goals and the aches of our heart, those things that if we were paid to stop talking about or doing we couldn't stop. Burdens will be bigger than ourselves and will always be about the greater good. If we have a burden to be rich or to see a group of people harmed, those are not burdens.

Hopefully, it is beginning to click that our stories were never meant to be just about us.

The third and final factor that is vital in connecting our stories with dreams and purposes is the recurring events in our lives. What are the events, types of people, situations, conversations, etc. that seem to recur in our lives? These are the situations we find ourselves constantly involved in without our planning. They are certain types of people or crowds we find ourselves mingling with or influencing. They are common phrases or comments that are said to us throughout our lives by different people.

My passions in life are encouraging, influencing, speaking, writing, exhorting and teaching others. My great burden is for people to walk unencumbered from their past, exploring possibilities in the present, while renewing lost dreams, visions, and hope for their future. Interestingly, the recurring events of my life are 1) being an African American woman put in leadership in predominantly white environments, 2) not fitting into the group or crowd, 3) being continually uprooted from locations, 4) being considered intimidating and distant.

Now, it's your turn to make a list of your passions, burdens and recurrences. Make three separate lists and write down as many in each category as you can think of from your past until now. Ask a friend or close acquaintance to help you with this exercise to provide feedback from their observations. Take as much time as you need to complete each category. As we begin to write our story the lists will become clearer.

You are going to need a journal book or notepad to continue with this exercise. This is for your eyes only, so be honest and real while writing. You decide how detailed you want to get with this exercise.

WRITING YOUR STORY

Writing out our story is the same as writing a great, exciting novel. As we begin, it is important to ask ourselves questions like, "What is my story?" "What does my story say about me?" "What have I learned from my story?" and "How am I going to use that story?"

We can now begin to create our story by combining our earliest memories, significant characters of our life, times of significant conflict or obstacles, what we learned or experienced, life-changing events, etc., and our resolution toward the future.

Here are some tips as we begin to write our stories out:

1. Try to write as objectively as possible. Our story is not about what others did or did not do. Our story is about what we experienced. Our story reveals a connection to the purpose of our life.

2. Cut to the chase. Write the story as though you were going to present it to a group and had five minutes to present it.

3. Do not undermine or judge your story because it lacks drama or has more worth than others because of the lack of drama. Your story is your story. It is impossible for anyone to compare stories regarding worth.

4. Your story should have a flow just like a well-written novel. Remember we are writing out a story that remains in the

process of a journey. None of us has arrived. The resolution is not an end but a location of your position in the journey at this point.

Our Background

Allow your mind to be an open slate. You can always go back and add events, people, and situations later. Keep in mind, writing your story is not an overnight process. It will take time. For now start to write down everything you can remember about your earliest memories. Write down any positive and negative memories you have as a baby or young child with your parents or siblings. The focus is the age and recollections, not the characters or your feelings. Simply try to recall your earliest memories and write them down, without judgment. Spend as much time as you need to finish. Here is an example:

Background:
- *Always in a hurry and by myself*
- *Wanted mother to love me*
- *Loved to dance with grandmother*
- *Loved grandparents*
- *Daydreamed a lot*
- *Enjoyed being at school with teachers*

A Time of Dreaming

Now begin to write out times from the past when you remember dreaming and being asked about your dreams and desires. Write out the dreams you recall having and the excitement of the moments. This will be a time when you recall sitting on a father's lap, playing with siblings and overall feeling safe and free.

Usually memories will be connected to our younger years of life as a child. As you recall this time in your life, try not to isolate a perfect time, but a segment of time when you were happy and had positive and enjoyable memories. You might also have some painful or conflicting memories during this time based on your home of origin. Try to think overall or "in the majority of time" when doing this part of the exercise.

As you continue to write out these aspects of your story, keep thinking about the content of a good novel. The only difference between the two is that your story is an autobiography that is continuing to be told.

Time of Dreaming:
- *Dreamed about having a family and a cat*
- *Stayed with grandparents & learned their values and sense of love & dreaming*
- *Had tea parties with my grandmother & made things in my Easy Bake Oven*
- *Felt protected by my grandfather*

The People We Knew

After you have exhausted your earliest memories and written them down, next begin to write down the significant people in your story that impacted your life positively or negatively. This will take some time, so be patient and don't rush it. Just list the people in your story, not how they affected you.

<u>People:</u>
- *Grandparents*
- *Mother*
- *Father*
- *Sisters, Brother*
- *Jazz musicians*
- *Abusers*
- *High school teacher*
- *Pastor*
- *Linda*

Difficulties or Obstacles

This part might begin to get a little difficult. Now begin to write out that time in your past when you found life difficult, painful, and challenging. This time connects our younger years of life to usually before our mid-twenties. It is usually a time or series of events that were traumatic or changed the way we viewed God, the world, and ourselves consciously or subconsciously. Don't think of difficulty in comparative terms. Try not to discount any loss, minor comment said, conflict, or point of difficulty simply because it does not seem dramatic or traumatic. Your story is your story!

As you try to recall this time, think in terms of segments instead of just events in your life when you were heartbroken, troubled, confused, conflicted, and can recall negative and painful memories. You might also have some enjoyable or positive memories during this time based on your home of origin. Try to think overall or "in the majority of time" when doing this part of the exercise.

Difficulties or Obstacles:

- *Abused between ages of 18 months and 16 years old*
- *Stopped dreaming*
- *College years of secrets and depression*
- *Words said by pastor*
- *Gained value and worth from my performance*
- *Learned tears and crying were wrong and weak, only strength and achievement is positive*

Discoveries

We now come to making a list of those things that happened during our journey of discovery and survival. This section should be uplifting and encouraging to write. Write down things you have discovered about yourself or did not realize before. Think about the situations of the previous section and the steps of the journey you went through to get on the other side or to learn more about why you felt the way you felt.

This section does not claim success that we have arrived, completed our recovery, no longer have issues, or have feelings about situations. Ask others to help you with this section if needed. Talk to people who have walked with you in your life and have seen the differences in you. Ask them how you've changed, grown, and reacted to situations differently.

Discoveries:

- *Learned worth, acceptance & love was based on my identity, not what I do*
- *Learned to place others before myself & compassion for hurting people*
- *See people as walking wounded on a level playing field. Not surprised by anyone's story because I know mine.*
- *Would redo life and experiences again because of what I've gained*

Resolution

Finally, this section pushes us to dream and look into the unknown. This section helps us discover things we longed for but perhaps placed on the shelf. List the things that your story is yet to tell and will be told by those you leave behind as your legacy. This part of your story will be vital when we put it all together. This list should be life changing.

Resolutions:

- *Global speaking, teaching, writing, and charitable organization to help people grab hold of purpose, possibilities, and potential*
- *Past did not predicate my future*
- *Hoped legacy: "After crossing her path I began to dream."*

TELLING YOUR STORY

Our stories give reasons why we are here. They are to be lived and earned so that at the end of our days, others' lives are impacted, we are changed, and a legacy is created because of the purpose served in using the story of our life.

You are not a writer, teacher, mother, sister, businessperson, struggling speaker who has a passion to speak into people's lives, or anyone by accident. The situations that happened in your past, the job loss, the great family, the divorce, successful business, confusion, harm and everything else are part of our stories for a purpose and plan.

Your story is to share and to remind others they are not walking this journey alone. That means no story is worthless or too small. Every story, regardless of situation, circumstance, loss, tragedy, or joy, is important. Someone could get off drugs or turn their life around because of your story. Someone could begin a business or begin a new life because of your story. Someone could even begin to dream again because of your story.

Your story is not meant for you to remain in pain or sorrow. It is to be used for greatness, for others, to tell, and for a purpose. There are those of you who were told you would never amount to anything. Others feel they are just a housewife or just a student or just a whatever. But in time, through your story you could be pouring into someone's life and witnessing them change beyond anything ever imagined. While we do not know all the reasons for our stories, we can be sure that there is a great purpose.

CHAPTER THIRTEEN

PURPOSE: LIVING A LIFE THAT MATTERS
"I believe God made me for a purpose, but he also made me fast. And when I run I feel His pleasure."

---- Eric Liddell (1902–1945)

One of my favorite quotes comes from John Adams. He said, "There are only two creatures of value on the face of this earth; those with a commitment and those requiring the commitment of others." His quote reminds us that our stories and dreams need to lead us to more. Hopefully, they lead us toward a commitment to make and/or the commitment others need to make.

A commitment is simply a pledge to do something or to offer someone. We have a commitment to make in seeing our dreams through to fruition. It is not enough to have a dream, hope, and walk through a process. A dreamer needs commitment to persevere and live it out. The dreamer also has a commitment to lead. An interesting thing happens to those who dream: People watch, follow them, and see those dreamers as people to be admired. The dreamer does not create a commitment from others, but people follow because of the example of courage and fortitude shown by the dreamer. I have never seen a dreamer walk through a journey without gaining followers to watch the movement toward a commitment.

A commitment drives us toward our goals. A commitment drives us toward our purpose. We can easily obtain a goal without a commitment. However, it is impossible to reach our potential, fullest possibilities, and our purpose with being committed.

PURPOSE

Often words like *purpose*, *potential*, and *calling* get mixed up in definition. While they have similar aspects, they are not the same. Our purpose is vital. It is something set up as an object or end to be attained.

It is important to know that our values and beliefs influence our purpose, which is similar to our goals. Purpose, however, goes much deeper and broader than a goal. Goals are the point or place we wish to achieve through a plan or action. They have specific targets that can be seen. We can measure our goals, check off accomplishments from the list, and establish specific, realistic objectives. None of those things is applicable regarding our purpose.

Unlike a goal, our purpose does not have a specific target or hold a time line or a deadline. It is not short or long term but only pertains to something personal and is deeply rooted in a person.

In some cases, a person's purpose will never be completed until their death. A purpose is not seen; it is experienced and ultimately known to the person. Our purpose is the reason we achieve a goal, and it cannot be measured. Our purpose gives meaning to our lives and allows us to feel as though we matter and have worth.

On any given day, I can sit in my cozy overstuffed chair, lean back and begin to dream about situations, positions, and events that I desire and hope to come true for my future. My dreams are never too big, crazy, or out of reach.

Not a day goes by that I don't imagine my place in front of thousands, reaching millions through the media to influence, motivate, impact, and exhort lives to Dream Madly, Pursue Wildly, and Trust Completely for a life that matters despite their past or present situations.

My dream is so large and so clear that I can write the details of what the venues look like. I can envision how many different books will be sold in the back of the room, the words I will speak, the staff I will have, the global extensions of the company, and the foundation that will help young people to recapture their dreams and hopes. I even know which days of the week I will schedule for down time. Like the dream of Martin Luther King, I can grasp it so clearly and passionately that time, not possibility, holds the promise of its coming to fruition.

My dream is a reflection of my passions, themes throughout my life, my burdens, my story, and my deepest desires. My dream gives an indication of how I am wired and how the events and journey of my life play into my purpose and potential. However, my dreams and purpose are not the same, nor do they evaluate the potential placed inside me.

When we are walking in our dreams, no matter how big or small, we often get a sense that our dream and purpose are the same because of the fulfillment. While our dream can include our purpose, it rarely contains our purpose.

For example, I have an acquaintance by the name of Scott. Scott possesses a gift of being a sanguine personality that lights up a room and makes everyone feel important and cared about. He truly is a man who could sell a glass of water to a drowning man. He loves the challenge and art of selling that gives him a sense of pride and worth, while mingling with people rather than a multitude of tasks.

For years, he worked in the air-conditioning and heating industry as a top salesperson. He excelled at his job and brought in a great deal of money to the company he worked for as a residential and commercial sales agent.

Scott had a simple dream that danced in his heart for years. He wanted to remain a salesperson in the same industry but work in an environment with his best friend and people he enjoyed. He dreamed to have a position where he could add value, be paid well, have autonomy, have a voice in the direction of the company without being a business owner, and that would allow him time to spend with his son.

Scott's dream was a reflection of his passion for selling, his burden to add value to others' lives, and his deepest desire to make a great living doing what he loves in an encouraging and flexible environment.

Today, Scott lives out his dream and feels blessed to daily wake to a life and career that he loves. Scott believes a great part of his purpose is to open avenues of learning and adventure to young people and to inspire them to become entrepreneurs and leaders who affect their communities. His dream gives an indication of how Scott is wired and expresses aspects of his potential but does not fully answer the purpose or calling of his life.

DREAMING, PURSUING, TRUSTING

The dream begins with Dreaming Madly. That is reclaiming those lost dreams, listening to the dreams and visions you have that seem totally crazy and out of reach. Putting fear aside, allowing yourself to hope and long for your wildest dreams for ministry, family, work, passions, and the use of the gifts, talents, and abilities you have been given.

Next comes our part in Pursuing Wildly. Everything is a choice and every pursuit has a cost. The cost for many of us is to finally let go. Letting go of the people we are still waiting for apologies and forgiveness to offer because of pain they caused in our past. Letting go of feelings that keep us trapped in believing we are not good enough, lovable enough, or acceptable enough or that we are the only ones who feel the bitter feelings we feel.

It is time to let go of equating our difficulty and obstacles with our feelings of being unusable. It's time to let go of the insanity that our past, our current situation, who we are or what we did is greater than the potential of our future. We must be willing to take the next courageous step of moving out of what is comfortable, risk-free, pain-free, and easy. Pursue what has been placed in you like a starving man in search of a meal.

Finally, Trust Completely. Not in our ability, gifts, talents, strength or even willingness to do. The greatness of possibility only comes from the source that we trust in and ultimately place our faith in. We must trust that we alone are the ones who are called to the specific dream or vision we have.

Our responsibility is to wait with hope and anticipation, continue to move, challenge, release, let go, and walk through those things and places in our path, and to Trust Completely in the midst of what looks like insanity to our mortal eyes.

LIVING A LIFE THAT MATTERS

A while ago, I was refreshed and greatly impacted by the words of my pastor. Although he stated the message was for him, the message spoke to me. It is a message that I believe addresses why it is vital to continue moving through to your dreams and toward your purpose in living a life that matters.

My pastor spoke of the fact that like Mary's virgin birth, similar miracles of birth happen inside us. He was referring to dreams, visions, projects, etc. that God impregnates in us that we are not able to do in our own ability and will always seem impractical, impossible, unknown and incredibly difficult. He was referring to natural dreams and hopes that we have longed for since childhood but failed to step out upon.

His message spoke to me because as I end this book, I realize there are many of you who are experiencing the pain of going into labor. You have traveled through experiences, pain, loss, difficulty, discouragement, directionlessness, frustration, fear and struggle to the point of wanting to shut down. You have tried to make your life work and pushed along wondering if you or having a dream is really worth the cost.

I encourage you to ponder this. Perhaps a dream, goal or vision that is unknown, difficult, and seems impossible to your eyes is being birthed in you for a reason, a purpose. Lord knows, you have or will experience times that cause you to wonder if you are losing your mind. Be encouraged. You are not crazy because things seem so difficult and trying. The closer you are to labor, the rougher it will be. The war will always be against your potential. The lies will always be in place simply to cut off your potential. The dream stealers will always be lurking to steal away your potential.

Whatever had been placed on your heart to do ... Do It! If you have been given a vision to pursue, you must follow through because you have been chosen in order for that vision to take place as designed. If you have a dream, please do not let me, dream stealers, employers, financial situations, depression, friends, Christians, busyness, life or anything else get in the way of grasping it as though it were your last breath.

I am convinced that the more difficult the journey, the greater the vision and the result. If your dream is easy and costs you nothing, give it up because it is not a dream, it is simply a task you completed. You can do this because your dream, your vision, your passion, your purpose is so worth the trouble.

At the end of your days, how do you desire to be remembered? As one who lived safely but had big dreams, or as one who lived courageously, pursing their dreams and visions yet fell short sometimes? As for me, I refuse to accept what is easily obtainable and safe in exchange for the great madness and pursuit of Dreaming Wildly.

I encourage you to view each day as a new opportunity to start fresh. It is easy to look at our past or our present situations and believe we are fated to failure or remain in the ordinary and hopeless. I encourage you not to believe the lies of what you feel but trust in the truth that is reality. Walk in courage, knowing nothing is impossible. You can do this!

To my fellow wind fliers: *"Do not allow those who prefer to dwell on the safe land of 'I won't' and 'It can't' to pull you down or discourage you. Continue to dream, asking, 'Why not?' knowing 'you will' in time. Soar so high that you only hear faint echoes of those on the land and you're only pushed forward by the wings ... of those flying among you."* – Charlotte D. Hunt

CHAPTER FOURTEEN

MESSAGES OF THE PAST

(THE PAST)

(MESSAGES RECEIVED)

(FEELINGS, EMOTIONS & BELIEFS)

(DREAM STEALERS)

Copyright © 2011 by Charlotte D. Hunt

MESSAGES OF THE PAST (Example)

(THE PAST)

Mother	Pastor	Abuse	Staying w/ grandparent	"I love you when…"	"God will never use you… damaged goods"

(MESSAGES RECEIVED)

Performance Weak	No future Damaged	No value	I'm loved Dream	No value work	Don't hope I'm wrong

(FEELINGS, EMOTIONS, & BELIEFS)

Unloved Frightened	Damaged	Used Worthless	Happy safe	unenjoyed	lost

(DREAM STEALERS)

Emotions Past	People Past	Past Emotions Addictions	N/A	Performance	Fear Emotions

Copyright © 2011 by Charlotte D. Hunt

Exercises and Worksheets

FEELING WORD LIST[2]

OPEN	HAPPY	ALIVE	GOOD
understanding	great	playful	calm
confident	cheerful	courageous	peaceful
reliable	joyous	energetic	at ease
easy	lucky	liberated	comfortable
amazed	fortunate	optimistic	pleased
free	delighted	provocative	encouraged
sympathetic	overjoyed	impulsive	clever
interested	gleeful	free	surprised
satisfied	thankful	frisky	content
receptive	important	animated	quiet
accepting	festive	spirited	certain
kind	ecstatic	thrilled	relaxed
	satisfied	wonderful	serene
	glad	jubilant	free and easy
	elated	sunny	bright
			blessed
			reassured

189

FEELING WORD LIST₂

LOVE	INTERESTED	HOPEFUL	STRONG
loving	concerned	eager	impulsive
considerate	affected	keen	free
affectionate	fascinated	earnest	sure
sensitive	intrigued	intent	certain
tender	absorbed	re-enforced	rebellious
devoted	inquisitive	inspired	unique
attracted	nosy	determined	dynamic
passionate	snoopy	excited	tenacious
admiration	engrossed	enthusiastic	hardy
warm	curious	bold	secure
touched		daring	brave
sympathy		hopeful	confident
close		challenged	
loved		optimistic	
comforted			

Exercises and Worksheets

FEELING WORD LIST 2

ANGRY	DEPRESSED	CONFUSED	HELPLESS
irritated	lousy	upset	incapable
enraged	disappointed	doubtful	alone
hostile	discouraged	uncertain	paralyzed
insulting	ashamed	indecisive	fatigued
sore	powerless	perplexed	useless
annoyed	diminished	embarrassed	inferior
upset	guilty	hesitant	vulnerable
hateful	dissatisfied	shy	empty
unpleasant	miserable	stupefied	forced
offensive	detestable	disillusioned	hesitant
bitter	repugnant	unbelieving	despair
aggressive	anxious	skeptical	frustrated
resentful	disgusting	distrustful	distressed
indignant	abominable	misgiving	woeful
provoked	terrible	lost	pathetic
incensed	in despair	unsure	tragic
infuriated	sulky	uneasy	in a stew
cross	bad	pessimistic	dominated

FEELING WORD LIST₂

INDIFFERENT	AFRAID	HURT	SAD
insensitive	fearful	crushed	tearful
dull	terrified	tormented	sorrowful
nonchalant	suspicious	deprived	pained
neutral	anxious	pained	grief
reserved	alarmed	tortured	anguish
weary	panic	dejected	desolate
bored	nervous	rejected	desperate
preoccupied	scared	injured	pessimistic
cold	worried	offended	unhappy
disinterested	frightened	afflicted	lonely
lifeless	timid	aching	grieved
	shaky	victimized	mournful
	restless	heartbroken	dismayed
	doubtful	agonized	a sense of loss
	threatened	appalled	
	cowardly	humiliated	
		wronged	
		alienated	

THE SURVEY

There is no right or wrong answer. This survey is for everyone regardless of religion, race, nationality, geography, political views, or marital status. Answer honestly, not based on what you think you should answer. No one will see your individual answers and your name will not be used. Feel free to use a fake name. This is for further research for my upcoming book only.

Directions: Please answer either True or False to the following statements of behaviors and beliefs. Think, "in most cases" or "often" when responding to the statements. Do not spend more than **5 seconds** to think about each statement. After you complete the survey

1. I am a good person because I do good things.
2. I can't trust people because I'll get hurt
3. I need things to go my way to be happy and content.
4. Others don't (clean, organize, handle situations, etc.) like I can so I need to do it to make sure it's right.
5. Life is better if I had significant other
6. When I am hurt or disappointed I feel I need to do something, eat or take something to feel better.
7. I would be okay if the abuse, trauma, hurt, etc. never happened.
8. I have worth because I impact people's lives and try to make a difference.

9. It is hard for me to have guilt-free fun or totally relax.
10. I am unhappy because of someone else in my life or my past.
11. Life should be fair.
12. People can't handle the real me.
13. It's better to hold in my emotions and anger than to let it all out.
14. If I don't do it, it won't get done.
15. Things will be better if I just try harder.
16. I offer advice to others to help them, even if they don't ask.
17. I have a tendency to take things personally.
18. I will never allow myself to be hurt like I was hurt before.
19. The problem is that I just need to have more faith (in whatever it may be).
20. I have unexplainable illnesses (i.e. headaches, stomach aches, etc.) that are not connected to a known disease that I have.
21. I need people to love me or accept me.
22. Either something is right or it is wrong. Either someone is good or they are bad.
23. I need to keep a wall up to protect myself and other people from getting hurt.
24. If I get a better handle or control my emotions, I will be alright.
25. I'm acceptable because I'm attractive, people like me and I take care of myself.

26. It is important to meet the emotional needs of others.
27. When I'm in a romantic relationship, I am usually the one taking charge.
28. I'm over my issues because I'm older or feel better
29. It's difficult to ask for help.
30. I usually feel less than or that there is something wrong with me.
31. I need to keep eyes on goal instead of enjoying journey.
32. I get jealous of others' happiness and success.
33. I can't be of great use unless I have it together and strong.
34. When I am not moving forward or my life is not working, I get sad, angry or depressed.
35. I use code to communicate. (Drop hints to get someone to do something or react)
36. I get hurt easily.
37. If I was doing things right, my life would be going better and I would not have struggles like I do.
38. I am successful because I have accomplished a lot.
39. I give in to things I don't want to do because I don't want to disappoint others
40. People like me because I go out of my way help people.
41. I am a bad person because I do bad things.
42. I worry about things all the time.
43. I am afraid to confront people who I think will reject me.
44. I often react based on how I feel.
45. It is better to be strong than vulnerable.

46. I am not successful, a good person, able to achieve great things, etc. because of my past or failures in my past.
47. I am afraid of being abandoned by people.
48. It is easy for me to get obsessive about things or people.
49. It's easy for me to find fault with myself and/or others.
50. I can't forgive people who have harmed me greatly
51. I am often dissatisfied.
52. I don't feel attractive unless I look like a model
53. I have no choice in matters
54. My life would be better if I had a mate
55. People can make me happy or sad
56. People really knew me they would abandon or reject me
57. Need to use my sexuality or looks to be acceptable
58. Crying, being vulnerable and talking to people about my problems is weak
59. I need love and acceptance from people
60. I am responsible for others emotional needs

REMINDERS OF THE TRUTH

1. You were born to dream
2. No matter how big or small, you are worth having a dream
3. Your story, no matter how bad or good, is for a purpose and to impact others
4. There is a plan and a destiny for you
5. Your past never disqualifies you from your future
6. What your father, mother, or person who told you that you couldn't said was and will ever be wrong
7. People, fear, performance, emotions and the past are only dream stealers if you allow them to be
8. Without being famous, wealthy, or in a position, your life and what you do is important
9. Your worth is NOT based on what you do, sell, earn, or have it is based on who you are alone
10. Your dreams are vital and worth following
11. Making a mistake or failing is not a disqualifier but an opportunity for growth and character…keep moving forward
12. A sign that you are walking your journey well is struggle and testing and others being impacted by watching you
13. You are good enough
14. You deserve more than being ordinary
15. Your feelings are NOT the truth only indicators of something

NOTES

Chapter One:
WHAT YOU WANTED TO BE WHEN YOU GREW UP

1. Dr. Charles P. Pollak, director of the Center for Sleep Medicine at NewYork-Presbyterian/Weill Cornell Medical Center, New York Times
   From article *"Do Babies Dream? World of Lucid Dreaming"*
   www.world-of-lucid-dreaming.com/do-babies-dream.html

2. "Mind-Body-Mood Advisor: Why You Should Breathe Like a Baby," by Jeffery Rossman, PhD. Rodale News, October 12, 2009. (www.rodale.com/diaphragmatic-breathing-and-health)

Chapter Two:
TO DREAM MADLY: THE PATH LESS TAKEN

1. Merriam-Webster Online Dictionary copyright © 2011 by Merriam-Webster (www.Merriam-Webster.com)

2. Merriam-Webster Online Dictionary copyright © 2011 by Merriam-Webster (www.Merriam-Webster.com)

3. National Institutes of Health. National Sleep Foundation. Reviewed by The Sleep Medicine Center at The Cleveland Clinic. © 2010 WebMD, LLC. All rights reserved.

Chapter Four:
DREAM STEALER #1-FEAR

1. Layton, Julia. "How Fear Works," September 13, 2005. HowStuffWorks.com. <http://health.howstuffworks.com/mental health/human-nature/other-emotions/fear.htm> 22 June 2011.

2. Michael Lewis, Director of the Institute for the Study of Child Development at Robert Wood Johnson Medical School in New Brunswick, N.J. from article "Factoring Fear: What Scares Us and Why" by Lou Dzierzak, October 27, 2008

3. Chillot, Rick. "What are you afraid of? 8 secrets that make fear disappear." Prevention, May 1998 v50 n5 p98 (7).

Chapter Five:
DREAM STEALER #2-THE PAST

1. Merriam-Webster Online Dictionary copyright © 2011 by Merriam-Webster (www.Merriam-Webster.com)

2. Rebecca Leung (2005-03-02). "Hilary Swank: Oscar Gold – 60 Minutes". CBS News. http://www.cbsnews.com/stories/2005/03/02/60II/main677647.shtml. Retrieved 2010-09-09

Chapter Six:
DREAM STEALER #3-EMOTIONS

1. Directed by Wachowski brothers, Produced by Joel Silver, Written by Wachowski brothers, Distributed by Warner Bros. Pictures, Release date North America: March 31, 1999

Notes

2. Merriam-Webster Online Dictionary copyright © 2011 by Merriam-Webster (www.Merriam-Webster.com)

3. "The Octave Of Primary Emotions", by Charles B. Parselle, May 2007, http://www.mediate.com/articles/parselle20.cfm

4. Difference Between Feelings and Emotions | Difference Between | Feelings vs Emotions http://www.differencebetween.net/miscellaneous/difference-between-feelings-and-emotions/#ixzz1RqECvDvH

5. Spiritual.com.au. "Emotions Pt2 – How we repress our emotions". Retrieved July 2010 from http://www.spiritual.com.au/articles/personal-development/emotions-repress-kurus2.htm

6. A List of Emotions Can Give Clarity to Our Feelings Copyright 2009-2011 choosing-life-my-way.com

Chapter Seven:
DREAM STEALER #4-PEOPLE

1. "I Can't Make You Love Me" Writers Mike Reid and Allen Shamblin, Producer, Bonnie Raitt and Don Was, Capitol Records Recorded 1990, Released October 22, 1991

2. Stillwell, Paul. *The Reminiscences of Master Chief Boatswain's Mate Carl Brashear.* Annapolis, MD: *United States Naval Institute.* 1998.

Chapter Eight:
DREAM STEALER #5-PERFORMANCE

1. Song Control, John McClain, Jimmy Jam and Terry Lewis, Janet Jackson, A&M August–October 1985 at Flyte Tyme Productions Studio in Minneapolis, Minnesota , **Released** February 6, 1986

Chapter Ten:
TRUSTING COMPLETELY: THE FREEDOM OF CHOICE

1. Merriam-Webster Online Dictionary copyright © 2011 by Merriam-Webster (www.Merriam-Webster.com)

Chapter Twelve:
A DREAM FROM YOUR STORY

1. Directed by Steven Spielberg, Produced by Ian Bryce, Mark Gordon Gary Levinsohn, and Steven Spielberg, Written by Robert Rodat, Distributed by DreamWorks Paramount Pictures, Release date United States: July 24, 1998

2. Merriam-Webster Online Dictionary copyright © 2011 by Merriam-Webster (www.Merriam-Webster.com)

3. Merriam-Webster Online Dictionary copyright © 2011 by Merriam-Webster (www.Merriam-Webster.com)

Chapter Thirteen:
EXERCISES & DIAGRAMS

1. www.psychpage.com/learning/library/assess/feelings.html

2. c) 2005 by Center for Nonviolent Communication, http://www.cnvc.org/Training/feelings-inventory , Website: www.cnvc.org

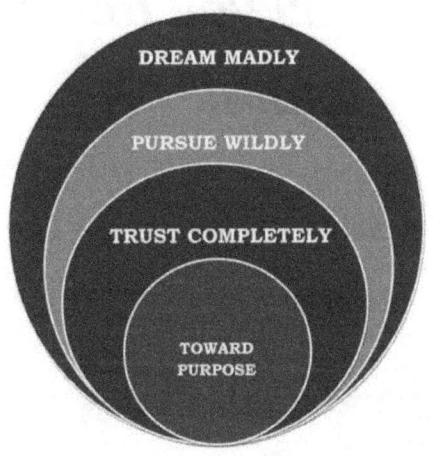

Check out our website at www.charlottehunt.com for booking information, products, mailing lists, and schedules

DREAM MADLY PROGRAMS
Plano, TX 75093

"No past or present situation can ever disqualify you from your future!"

This award-winning book was featured on The 700 Club.

"This is the best book I have read since the Bluest Eye, by Toni Morrison. This page-turner is encouraging, heart warming, and inspiring. I recommend it for everyone to read. It doesn't matter whether your story is similar or totally different you will feel empowered after reading Damaged Goods."

Tammy Curry, LSC, Awareness4Life Coach

Based on the author's miraculous journey, "DAMAGED GOODS: An Autobiography" is an amazingly uplifting, funny, transforming and life-changing story of an invitation to recall and read through her life to reveal her potential and purpose.

**AVAILABLE ONLINE AT
WWW.CHARLOTTEHUNT.COM**

ABOUT THE AUTHOR

Known to those she mentors as "the gentle taskmaster who helps people dream again," Charlotte Hunt is the founder of Dream Madly, designed to help organizations and individuals dream madly, pursue wildly, and trust completely toward their dreams and potential despite their past and in the midst of today's problems through presentations, workshops, books, and resources.

Charlotte has spoken and performed before audiences of celebrities, political figures, world-renowned musical artists, dignitaries, leaders, educators, psychologists, survivors of abuse, prison inmates, addicts, the hopeless, and everyone in between exhorting them to fulfill their purpose and potential.

From the beginnings of a tragic past starting at the age of eighteen months and a curse on her future and God's use from a pastor's lips, her life has endured great trials, suffering, and struggles. Despite the many setbacks, hardship and tragedies, she succeeded through faith, hope, and perseverance to become an international runway model, recording jazz artist, touring actress, national radio personality, award-winning author, counselor, organizational consultant and global inspirational speaker helping thousands to reclaim their potential, purpose, and dreams in learning to "Dream Madly, Pursue Wildly, and Trust Completely"™.

www.ingramcontent.com/pod-product-compliance
Lightning Source LLC
Chambersburg PA
CBHW031640040426
42453CB00006B/164